Where GREAT Teaching BEGINS

Where GREAT Teaching BEGINS

Planning for Student Thinking and Learning

Anne R. Reeves

Alexandria, Virginia USA

1703 N. Beauregard St. • Alexandria, VA 22311-1714 USA
Phone: 800-933-2723 or 703-578-9600 • Fax: 703-575-5400
Website: www.ascd.org • E-mail: member@ascd.org
Author guidelines: www.ascd.org/write

Gene R. Carter, *Executive Director;* Judy Zimny, *Chief Program Development Officer;* Gayle Owens, *Managing Director, Content Acquisitions & Development;* Scott Willis, *Director, Book Acquisitions & Development;* Genny Ostertag, *Acquisitions Editor;* Julie Houtz, *Director, Book Editing & Production;* Katie Martin, *Editor;* Reece Quiñones, *Senior Graphic Designer;* Mike Kalyan, *Production Manager;* Keith Demmons, *Typesetter*

Printed in the United States of America. Cover art © 2011 by ASCD. ASCD publications present a variety of viewpoints. The views expressed or implied in this book should not be interpreted as official positions of the Association.

All web links in this book are correct as of the publication date below but may have become inactive or otherwise modified since that time. If you notice a deactivated or changed link, please e-mail books@ascd.org with the words "Link Update" in the subject line. In your message, please specify the web link, the book title, and the page number on which the link appears.

ASCD Member Book, No. FY12-2 (Nov. 2011, PSI+). ASCD Member Books mail to Premium (P), Select (S), and Institutional Plus (I+) members on this schedule: Jan., PSI+; Feb., P; Apr., PSI+; May, P; July, PSI+; Aug., P; Sept., PSI+; Nov., PSI+; Dec., P. Select membership was formerly known as Comprehensive membership.

PAPERBACK ISBN: 978-1-4166-1332-9   ASCD product # 111023
Also available as an e-book (see Books in Print for the ISBNs)

Quantity discounts for the paperback edition only: 10–49 copies, 10%; 50+ copies, 15%; for 1,000 or more copies, call 800-933-2723, ext. 5634, or 703-575-5634. For desk copies: member@ascd.org.

Library of Congress Cataloging-in-Publication Data

Reeves, Anne R.
  Where great teaching begins : planning for student thinking and learning / Anne R. Reeves.
      p. cm.
  Includes bibliographical references and index.
  ISBN 978-1-4166-1332-9 (pbk. : alk. paper) 1. Instructional systems–Design. 2. Effective teaching. I. Title.
  LB1028.38.R44 2011
  371.33–dc23
                            2011030262

20 19 18 17 16 15 14 13 12 11   1 2 3 4 5 6 7 8 9 10 11 12

Where GREAT Teaching BEGINS

Planning for Student Thinking and Learning

Acknowledgments

Thanks to Charles Ragland, who planted the seed for this book in 2004 by working with me to create readings for a course in instructional design. In the ensuing years, he has stimulated, challenged, and supported my thinking about planning and the ideas that underlie it.

Thanks also to Jessamyn and David, who provided feedback as readers and specific editorial advice on drafts of the early chapters. Their insight, aid, and encouragement were invaluable.

And finally, thanks to the many education students who have shown me—through questions, trial and error, trial and success, and their own early teaching—what they need in order to understand, create, and use well-designed instruction.

Introduction

Have you ever watched a child play school? Maybe you remember playing school yourself—lining up your younger siblings or teddy bears on the floor while you stood in front of them, taking charge. You, or the child you've watched, probably demonstrated most of the visible aspects of what teaching involves: directing, praising, reprimanding, asking questions, explaining things, and generally engaging in the routines of classroom life. Teaching is understood to be a performance with a script—a script that leaves some room for improvisation but repeatedly pulls the actors back to traditional routines. What is both fascinating and alarming about this script is that a teacher can perform it quite proficiently without generating much learning in students' minds.

In a wonderful essay reflecting on a long career spent investigating student learning, Graham Nuthall (2005) noted that, whatever the formal curriculum might be, students learn about classrooms and about what teachers do from their own experience of being students. Those students who grow up to become teachers themselves tend to put this learning into practice. Nuthall described "ritualized routines" (p. 895) of classroom teaching that are carried on generation after generation and based primarily on principles of classroom management. Many of the teachers he observed had learned to be pleased with their lessons when they could see students demonstrating engagement and cooperating with the requirements of the assigned activities. Significantly, Nuthall noted that the primary focus for both students and teachers was task completion. Both groups measured the success of a lesson more by how well students had carried out classroom activities than by what students had learned from the activities.

In my own experience as a student, a teacher, and a teacher-educator, I have seen for myself exactly what Nuthall described. I grew up seeing teaching as a matter of keeping order, delivering information, assigning tasks and projects, and giving tests. Like so many of my peers, I internalized these behaviors—this performance—as being "What Teaching Is."

This ritualized-routine approach to teaching is no longer tenable in this age of instructional accountability, in which attention to individual students' learning has become a priority. We need to understand that for any given assignment, some of our students may be going through the motions—not engaging in the cognitive activity necessary to expand their knowledge base—while others may be reviewing information they already know. We need to confront the fact that too many students are thinking of their classwork not as a route to learning but as tasks to be gotten out of the way, and too many teachers are out of touch with the cognitive development that we hope and assume is occurring in our students' minds. If what we think of as good teaching, even teaching that embodies "best practices," does not necessarily result in our students learning, what are teachers and teacher-educators to do?

In his essay, Nuthall focused on the "cultural myths" that schoolchildren absorb and that teachers perpetuate about teaching practices, and perhaps it was because his attention was so focused on the events that could be observed and measured in classrooms that he did not directly address planning and designing instruction. Yet if we are to challenge these myths and the practices that ensue from them, we must begin at the beginning of teaching, which is in the design of the whole instructional experience. And designing effective instruction requires educators to shift our attention from *teacher performance*—what the teacher does—to *student learning*—the intellectual work that students engage in and the outcome of that work.

In the more than 20 years I have been an educator, including the 12 that I have spent as an educator of teachers, I have seen that the most challenging feature of instructional design is creating objectives that focus on appropriate student learning instead of on classroom activities. I remember vividly how, as a beginner, I, too, lacked clarity about the purpose and practice of instructional design. My own early lesson planning efforts were superficial and tentative—not to mention of unpredictable effectiveness. I felt as though I were groping in a misty half-light, hoping that my next step would be the right one but not knowing how to tell whether it was or not. The only guidance available came from my students, who either learned what I intended for them to learn or did not—and, often, the nature and depth of their learning was only partly visible to me. Furthermore, I couldn't tell whether anything that I had done was responsible for my students' learning or if they had acquired skills and understanding from some other source.

Today, I see my own teacher-education students and many active teachers making those same uncertain gestures, guessing about the "right" way to frame objectives, assessments, and learning activities. Although education students take courses in instructional design and inservice teachers attend workshops and conferences that address selected details of instructional design, without a firm grasp of the purpose of instructional design, the details of how to plan lessons often presented in these classes, workshops, and conferences will simply be piled on top of a faulty conceptual foundation, and the desired outcomes of instruction will not be reliably achieved.

My own preservice education students have shown me, through their trials, mistakes, questions, and confusions, that they need to begin with the foundations of instructional design. So that is where this book begins.

I have also learned through experience that simply telling students things like "Objectives describe learning outcomes" or "Planning is necessary for coherent instruction" will produce nods of agreement but not necessarily the changes that will lead to more effective instructional design practices. Although my students' agreement may be real, basic shifts in perspective are difficult to bring about and require both time and practice. That is why the process of thinking about teaching and learning, for most people, must be taken in small steps, with many examples to illustrate the principles involved.

This book is not intended to provide an exhaustive account of everything that is important about designing instruction. Fortunately, many valuable sources of information are available about effective instructional and assessment methods to use in the classroom. The missing piece for today's teachers is a detailed account of how to establish the clear, effective learning objectives that will support subsequent sound decisions about instruction and assessment. For this reason, most of the emphasis in this book is on establishing objectives and all the thinking and conceptual understanding that underlies that work. Every teacher must know how to think about and carry out the detailed, step-by-step process of identifying outcomes for the whole teaching-and-learning enterprise.

Instructional design may seem deceptively easy to beginners. How hard can it be to figure out how to teach class tomorrow? Of course, once novice instructional designers grasp what the work really entails, the process can appear newly labyrinthine and mysterious—full of false starts and opportunities for error. It's natural to keep reverting to the teacher's classroom performance instead of attending to student learning outcomes because—and my students have made this clear over and over again—our experience has taught us what teachers do in a classroom, but it has given us very little information about what students should learn and how they should learn it. As students, we knew which of our peers answered questions correctly, but we did not otherwise pay much attention to what anyone was (or was not) learning. As students, many of us did not even pay much attention to our own learning, because the routines of school encouraged us to focus on getting assignments done in a way that pleased the teacher. For that we were rewarded, whether we learned anything meaningful or not.

Beginning instructional designers legitimately do not know what their instructional objectives are, much less how to state them clearly and "correctly." When they are far enough along in the process of shifting their focus to student learning to grasp how much they really don't know, they are like youngsters learning to ride a bicycle. Wobbling across the empty parking lot with a death-grip on the handlebars, they are aware that however fiercely they hang on, the whole project could still crash. These fledging planners wonder how it's possible to do what their expert colleagues do—create lesson after lesson, day after day, knowing what to say and do so that students learn what they should learn. But once the skill of effective instructional design is developed and practiced sufficiently, once balance is attained and forward momentum is brought under control, the work begins to come naturally and seem essential. The question shifts from "How can I possibly do this well?" to "What was so hard about that?" The purpose of this book is to help every reader "hop aboard" the practice of effective instructional design and move forward with increasing confidence and success.

1

Instructional Design: Who and What Is It For?

Visualize a teacher at work. What do you see?

Most of us imagine a person standing in front of a group of students, talking to them, giving them information, demonstrating something, asking questions, or monitoring group work or seatwork. Those of us who are teachers might also picture ourselves at our desk or at our own kitchen table, grading a stack of papers.

It is natural to think about teaching in terms of performance in front of the class. As children, we absorbed an understanding of what teachers do from what we experienced as students in the classroom. We were aware of teachers' delivery of information, their interactions with us and our fellow students, and the activities or assignments they required us to do. We were certainly aware of teachers' role as evaluators. What we were generally not aware of, though, was the work our teachers did to plan *what we would learn* and *how we would learn it*.

Here's an alternative picture of a teacher at work: a woman is sitting at a table with a few colleagues, pen in hand, laptop open, surrounded by textbooks, journals, magazines, and three-ring binders filled with teaching materials, including copies of state academic standards and the district's curriculum. This teacher and her colleagues are talking about a unit on the local community that they are in the process of planning. Together, they are exploring ways to bring social studies, English, science, math, and art into this unit—working to design instruction that will lead their 7th graders to achieve the grade-level curriculum learning goals. They are thinking less about their own performances than about what will be going on inside their students' minds. They are asking, "How can we translate the requirements of the state's academic standards into specific examples that will make sense to our students? What are the students ready to learn? What will engage them? What will they remember in the weeks, months, and years following this unit? How can we design this unit to be an effective, useful, and meaningful learning experience for them? How can we describe this plan in clear, precise, concise statements that will keep teachers and students on track throughout the unit?"

This is the "deep work" of teaching: designing instruction that takes teachers deep into content and deep into consideration of their students' learning. And although this example shows teachers planning collaboratively, it may be done just as effectively by individual teachers. What makes this approach to instructional design successful is that it goes far beyond selecting activities and writing tests; it extends past the teacher's performance to address the bedrock of the whole educational enterprise—demonstrated student learning.

The term "deep design" is intended to distinguish student- and learning-centered lesson planning from the classroom-centered, activity-oriented planning that is common among beginning teachers. Deep design work is not directly visible to students or to anyone else who is not part of it. Preservice and novice teachers may be only somewhat aware of its existence and its importance. It is based not on questions of "What will I do Monday morning?" or "What activity will my students enjoy?" but on questions of what and how students will learn, and how teachers and other education stakeholders will know that students have learned.

Figure 1.1 contrasts the extremes of these two approaches to instructional design.

Figure 1.1 • Contrasting Views of Instructional Design

Teacher- and Classroom-Centered Instructional Design	Student- and Learning-Centered Instructional Design
Focus on activities	Focus on what kinds of thinking students do
Focus on teacher performance	Focus on intellectual skills students develop
Focus on classroom events and experiences	Focus on what students take away from the classroom events and experiences
Burning question: "What will we be doing today?"	Burning question: "What will students be learning today?"
Planning addresses only the teacher's time with students	Planning addresses long-term outcomes

The visible parts of a teacher's job—the instructing, assigning, organizing, and assessing—are not easy to do, but their functions and importance are obvious. But because the teacher's planning for every student's learning is not so visible, it's harder to explain who and what such planning is for. New teachers, or teachers who have not been trained to design instruction in the deepest sense, may reasonably assume that planning is for teachers; it tells the teacher what to do. Or they may see planning as something done for administrators, who want to ensure that every teacher has a plan in place to address state academic standards. The idea of planning being for students' benefit might be last on the list—or missing from it altogether.

This book provides a step-by-step look at the process of designing instruction that is centered on student learning. As we begin, let us consider some immediate questions you may have.

"Is Deep Design Really Necessary?"

A teacher whose official success is measured in terms of students' strong test scores and the satisfaction of students, parents, and administrators may feel that there is no need to engage in deep design if current planning practices get good results. It is true that results are the measure of success. However, at any time, individual students may experience difficulties that will require the teacher to focus more intently on their learning. Deep design will equip a teacher to tackle this challenge.

Even when all is going well, you can deepen your understanding of your own practice by asking questions like

• What assumptions about student learning underlie my choice of activities?

• Can I explain the learning goals I have for students?

• Do I explain to students the kinds of thinking and intellectual skills that my activities require?

• Am I confident that I am maximizing the development of long-term skills and knowledge in each and every student?

These questions direct attention to the true goals of education, which begin in the classroom but ultimately lie beyond it. The benefit of shifting the planning focus to deep design is that looking at the bigger picture of what you and your students are doing—and why you are doing it—prepares you to explain to students, colleagues, and other stakeholders how your instruction will lead to lasting student learning.

If you currently use an activity-centered planning approach and feel satisfied that it is working well for your students, you may find it interesting to apply the tests of good design described later in this book to your plans. It's possible that student learning outcomes are driving your instruction after all. If so, it is likely that you are naturally aligning the elements of teaching—planning, instructing, and assessing—with state academic standards and your students' readiness to learn. Many good teachers operate effectively on their instincts and common sense. But the only way to get the most out of your instructional design is to examine it in detail. And you cannot share your good design practices with colleagues, parents, and students unless you have identified and articulated those practices.

There is one more thoroughly practical benefit of focusing on student learning rather than on activities: more effective time management. When an activity takes less time than anticipated, an activity-focused teacher must either search for ways to fill the remaining class period or give students free time. A learning-focused teacher will be glad to have a few extra minutes to develop students' knowledge further. That teacher might ask the students to explain what they have learned or to describe its connection to other topics in or aspects of the curriculum—and will almost always be rewarded with responses that show students to be up to the new challenges.

"Doesn't Deep Design Require More Work and Take More Time?"

Without question, deep design will be more work for teachers who are accustomed to begining and ending lesson planning by deciding what they and their students will do in class. But activity planning alone is superficial, unfinished planning. Determining what and how students will learn and how they will demonstrate their learning are not extra steps to be added but necessary steps that cannot be skipped.

The good news is that when your instructional design begins with a focus on students and then moves to classroom activities and your own performance, it does not need to take more time or effort. In fact, once you're sure of the desired learning outcomes, you'll often be able to map out the route to achieving them through activities more quickly. In short, when you shift your thinking to student learning, you are engaging in *smarter* planning, not more difficult planning.

"Doesn't the Teacher's Focus Belong on What Happens in the Classroom?"

Since so much of a teacher's professional life "happens" in a classroom with students, it can be disconcerting to focus on aspects of the job that do not involve actual classroom activity. Of course you must put a great deal of attention and energy into what you do with your students, but this is not an either/or situation. Deep design does not remove classroom-activity planning from the design process; it simply shifts activity planning to a later point in the process.

A teacher may also resist the idea of planning with students' long-term knowledge in mind because the shift in focus it requires can feel overwhelming. Classroom events are more or less under the teacher's control, but the responsibility for student learning that endures beyond the classroom is a heavier load to bear. Nonetheless, preparing students for their futures should be at the heart of every teacher's classroom work. With the right approach, we can *all* do this—and do it well.

"But This Kind of Planning Does Not Describe What the Teacher Should *Do!*"

It's true that student-centered instructional design does not necessarily tell teachers everything they need to do in a class. However, focusing on the students, their intellectual work, and the desired end point of their learning will make it easier to see what *should* happen in class. Knowing where the instruction is headed in the long term is essential to understanding what to do in the short term.

Even more to the point, a lesson plan or unit plan is not a schedule of events or an agenda for a teacher to follow. Its purpose is not to document what must be done, minute by minute, class period by class period, but to document what students must achieve. In other words, the goal of effective instructional design is to record the designer's conceptual plan for student learning and, as such, it answers certain key questions:

- What will students learn?
- To what degree will they learn? To what depth and breadth?
- How will they acquire this learning?
- How will they demonstrate this learning?

This approach to instructional design does *not* necessarily answer the more specific kinds of questions properly addressed in teacher's schedule or agenda, such as

- When will I collect homework?
- How will I prepare students for tomorrow's assembly?
- What will I do about students who missed the last test?
- How will I form student groups for this lesson?

Such step-by-step instructions for what to do and when to do it must be prepared and maintained, but the schedule for these steps becomes clear only after the design for learning has been created.

"So Who Are Lesson Plans Really For?"

Lesson plans are for you, the teacher. They map out what learning activities you will conduct in the classroom, what materials you will need, and what assessments you will give. Lesson plans are also for your administrators. They inform administrators of how you will go about addressing academic standards and preparing students for standardized tests. Ultimately, though, lesson plans are for students. When well-designed, lesson plans tell teachers and administrators how to generate, support, and assess *students'* learning. Any lesson plan that does not focus on student learning is incomplete.

In chapters to come, we will examine the elements of good design and work through the steps of creating effective, learning-focused instruction.

2

Objectives as the Foundation for Learning-Focused Instruction

The images that come up when we think of teaching and learning tend to be images of classroom activities. Such activities may be quietly conducted by individual students, such as independent reading and writing, or they may be social and noisy, like games and skit rehearsals. Because activities are the structures by which students learn, they must be selected and designed with great care. What makes an activity a good one for a particular course or group of students? How do you know what the students should be doing?

The answer is that you know what students should be doing based on the objectives you've established for their instruction. Instructional objectives are *statements of what students will know and be able to do at the end of the lesson or unit of instruction.* They describe the *learning outcomes for students* that the lesson is designed to produce. Once the objectives have been created, any activities that will help student achieve those objectives can be said to be the "right" activities.

Without objectives, you can't know whether or not your activities are appropriate. Even if you believe that creating formal objectives for each lesson is unnecessary, you almost certainly have a sense of what each lesson is intended to achieve. If you have learned from experience which activities will help your students learn particular content, you have internalized the objectives with which those activities are aligned.

Consider your own process of selecting instructional activities. If the criteria you use are limited to how engaging activities are for students, how much time they take, or what materials they require, then the actual goal that you are working toward is that activities be engaging, efficient, or easily conducted. Perhaps you have "inherited" activities from other teachers, which is the basis of your acceptance of these activities as valid uses of class time. These are all important considerations, but they are secondary to students' skill development and knowledge acquisition. If you begin planning by selecting appealing activities and *then* try to find standards or curriculum points they might meet, you're in danger of leaving entire sections of the curriculum unaddressed. Better to establish standards-based learning outcomes first and then look for ways to make that learning interesting, feasible, and manageable.

Let's take a look at an example. Suppose you are a member of the middle school team planning the community-investigation unit described in Chapter 1. You live in Texas, where the state's academic standards require 7th graders to learn something about economics. Your team is wondering how to incorporate economics instruction into your unit, and someone suggests that students take a walking tour of the main business district in town. Students could get acquainted with local businesspeople and talk to them about the town's economic activity. The objective underlying this activity might be written like this:

> *Students will take a walking tour to meet local businesspeople and learn some of the economic history of the town.*

As we get deeper into a discussion of objectives, we will see that this particular objective is inadequate for several reasons. For now, though, let us consider it from an activity-centered point of view and then from a student-learning point of view.

From the activity-centered viewpoint, this objective describes clearly enough what the lesson planner expects students to get from the activity: they will meet people and learn from them. From a student-learning viewpoint, however, it falls short. Think about what must happen for this objective to be "met." Students need to (1) go on the walking tour, (2) meet some businesspeople, and (3) learn some of town's economic history. Note that only the third and final part of this objective describes student learning, and the learning it describes is very general—vague, even. We can't tell, based on this objective, what students will learn from the businesspeople, what they will be able to do with whatever they learn, or whether or not what they learn will have any relation to the state academic standards focused on economics.

There are few more potential problems to consider. What if the students already know most of the local businesspeople and do not understand how to gain anything new from visiting these establishments and talking with the people who work there? What if the businesspeople that the students meet don't know much about the town's economic history and don't have any information to share? Or what if the businesspeople they speak with are poor teachers who generate confusion, pontificate about politics, or spread misinformation?

A teacher who is thinking carefully about student learning will need to identify certain conditions that must be met for this activity to be a good learning experience:

• Students need—but do not yet have—the information that the tour will provide.

• The sources of information are appropriate for students.

• The cost of the activity in time and effort is worth the value it contributes to students' learning.

- Students will absorb and remember the information presented to them.

This activity would definitely need to be researched and carefully planned to make sure it meets these conditions for student learning, and the objective would need to be clarified to ensure that student learning is its focus.

As you and your unit-planning teammates continue your development work, several learning objectives for this tour could emerge from the general original objective. If, for example, you identify the state standard "Explain the changes in the types of jobs and occupations that have resulted from the urbanization of Texas" (Texas Department of Education, 2010) as your target, a logical objective might be

> *Students will explain how five or more local businesses have come into existence as a result of urbanization.*

This objective would pertain to the particular lesson involving the students' interactions with local businesspeople, but other unit objectives could also draw on information the students would gain from those conversations, such as

> *Students will contrast urban and agrarian occupations in Texas using a variety of sources.*

Contrasting these more specific, learning-focused and standard-based objectives with the original clarifies how planning based solely on activities can often be incomplete. Until you first probe these activities for their learning value and then clearly identify that value, you cannot predict what the learning outcome of an activity will be. And unless you introduce standards into these planning considerations, you will not know what the learning outcome *should* be.

Thinking Beyond Classroom Activities

Although it is natural to visualize your teaching in terms of the instruction you will deliver and the activities your students will participate in, establishing instructional objectives requires you to visualize and define what students will know and be able to do after the lesson rather than what they'll be doing during it. Making this mental shift from *during* to *after* can be difficult, especially for novice teachers (or novice planners), who tend to fall back into the common practice of describing objectives for classwork rather than objectives for the learning that students will acquire from the lesson:

> *Students will take notes from a PowerPoint lecture about the stock market crash of 1929.*
>
> *Students will practice drawing squares, triangles, and circles.*
>
> *Students will complete a vocabulary worksheet.*

None of these statements about what students will do actually tells us what students will *learn*. Rather than describe learning outcomes, these objectives describe learning activities: taking notes, practicing drawing geometric figures, and completing a worksheet. Perhaps completing these activities will result in student learning, but perhaps not. And because none of these activities is necessarily the end of the learning process, they are not suitable as objectives.

Now contrast the original objectives with the following, revised to describe actual student learning outcomes:

> *Students will explain causes and effects of the stock market crash of 1929.*
>
> *Students will name and create squares, triangles, and circles.*
>
> *Students will match German words to their English translations.*

It's easy to mistake learning activities for learning outcomes. Underlying this mistake is the natural assumption that certain experiences automatically lead to certain learning. In other words, anyone doing x must learn y. The planner states the objective as x because, in the planner's mind, the learning is built into the doing. Listening to a lecture about causes of the 1929 stock market crash has to result in learning the causes the 1929 stock market crash, doesn't it? If only teaching and learning were that easy.

Stating an objective as "Students will do x" when the outcome you really want is "Students will learn y and demonstrate that learning" can lead to incomplete or even nonexistent learning. For example, if the plan for class is for students to play a game that requires mental addition and subtraction, a novice teacher might describe the objective like this:

> *Students will play a math game to practice their addition and subtraction skills.*

The teacher's assumption is that kids like games, they will engage in this one, and playing the game will automatically improve students' math skills. Although the emphasis in this objective is on playing the game, the teacher's true goal is this:

> *Students will be able to accurately add and subtract double-digit numbers.*

Here's another example. A science teacher takes her students outside to explore a meadow adjacent to the school property. The teacher's general goal is to impress upon students the diversity of plant and animal life in that meadow. She believes allowing them to discover this diversity for themselves in an authentic environment will make for a powerful and memorable learning experience. Her objective might be stated as follows:

> *Students will discover diversity in a meadow by coming face to face with it.*

What does this objective focus on—the learning activity or the desired learning? It focuses on the learning opportunity: exploring the meadow habitat. The teacher's assumptions are (1) that the students' participation in this activity will lead them to grasp that there is great diversity of life in the meadow, and (2) that their personal experience of this diversity will enlarge and enrich their understanding in unspecified ways. The teacher may reasonably feel that she is achieving this objective just by bringing students to the meadow.

What the teacher is probably not considering is the possibility that some students will not think and learn in the way she assumes they will. When they come face to face with goldenrod and rabbits, they might be thinking about any number of things besides the diversity of life in the meadow. Even if students *do* think about the flora and fauna they see, who's to say they will think about the flora and fauna in a way that meets the teacher's instructional goals? What if the students return to class and announce that what they discovered is that "The bees were really annoying, but we saw the cutest baby bunny and an awesome snake"?

Imagine the science teacher changes the objective to this:

> *Students will describe at least 12 plant species and 12 animal species found in the meadow.*

Better. With this revision, the teacher and the students will be looking for and recording a specific level of biological diversity. But this instructional objective describes fairly basic learning. If the teacher wants students to understand the relationships between the forms of life that make up a complex ecosystem, additional instructional objectives are necessary—perhaps something like these:

> *Students will explain the trophic levels of these 24 plant and animal species.*

> *Students will describe the biogeochemical cycle of carbon in this ecosystem.*

Instructional objectives can be written to describe whatever level of knowledge and thinking you want your students to engage in, from the simplest kind of intellectual activity to the most complex.

Helpful Techniques for Isolating Learning Outcomes

A straightforward way to focus an objective on student learning outcomes is to add the phrase "at the end of this lesson" (or "at the end of this unit") to it and then consider whether or not it still makes sense. Let's try it with three of the activity-centered objectives we looked at earlier:

> At the end of this lesson, *students will take notes from a PowerPoint lecture.*

> At the end of this lesson, *students will practice drawing squares, triangles, and circles.*

> At the end of this lesson, *students will complete a vocabulary worksheet.*

The note taking in the first of these three objectives is obviously an in-class learning activity, and practicing geometric shapes might be, too. The third objective we might be less certain about. Would completing the vocabulary worksheet constitute an application of newly acquired vocabulary knowledge, or would it be an in-class practice activity? The matter would be clearer if the object stated specifically which learning goal the activity (completing the worksheet) will serve. For example:

> *Students will match German words to their English translations*

> or

> *Students will complete sentences by selecting appropriate vocabulary words*

> or

> *Students will identify prefixes, roots, and suffixes in vocabulary words.*

These revised objectives focus on what students will know and be able to do rather than on the activities that the teacher will assign. If you add the phrase "at the end of this lesson" to the objective and the result is a statement that still makes sense, you are probably thinking of a true objective rather than classroom practice.

Try adding the "at the end of" prefix to the learning-centered objectives describing the community-exploration unit:

> At the end of this lesson, *students will explain how five or more local businesses have come into existence as a result of urbanization.*
> At the end of this unit, *students will contrast urban and agrarian occupations in Texas using a variety of sources.*

See how both these objectives clearly describe how students will use specific knowledge gained from the lessons to demonstrate their learning?

Another exercise that can help you focus on what a learning objective really describes is to imagine that students are leaving class at the end of the lesson that you are planning. The principal, a few parents, or maybe members of the school board are standing in the hall just outside the classroom. As the students go by, these adults stop them to ask, "What did you learn in there? What can you do now that you couldn't do before?" Ideally, the students will be able to say things such as

- "I can describe the process of photosynthesis."
- "I can explain how Holden Caulfield loses his innocence in *The Catcher in the Rye*."
- "I can define *dividend* and *multiplicand*."

These statements describe the outcomes of the intellectual work the students have done during class—their thinking about the topic, how they've made sense of it by connecting it to what they already know, and how they are remembering it. Thus, these statements are the teacher's and the students' learning objectives. The fact that students can now do these things, after instruction, shows that they have achieved the objectives.

As mentioned, some confusion about *during* instruction and *after* may arise when in-class practice is necessary to achieve the objectives. You could argue that there is no clear distinction between what students do during the lesson and what they do after the lesson if, for example, they practice reciting multiplication facts in class and then go home and recite the same multiplication facts to their parents. It is true that the students may demonstrate knowledge via the same activity they engaged in during class, but there is an important conceptual distinction between practice and achievement. Practice occurs *during learning,* while achievement is *demonstrated knowledge.* Objectives describe achievement, not practice. The students' behavior might be the same—reciting math facts—but when objectives are clearly understood, both teacher and learner can make this distinction, and the likelihood that students will achieve the objective is increased.

If you are still unsure about making the move from in-class activities to after-the-fact achievement, apply the principle of objectives to everyday life. Think about something you have accomplished: a problem solved, a task completed, a trip taken, games played, meals prepared, and so on. The objective for Thanksgiving dinner, for example, is to provide an enjoyable meal for family and friends. You may think more about the planning, shopping, cooking, and table-setting than you do about the actual eating of the meal, but your objective is to get good food on the table at the right time so that everyone eats a delicious holiday meal together. The pre-dinner activities are the means of getting there; they are not the objective itself.

This Thanksgiving example brings up another point of possible confusion about distinguishing between *during* the achievement of the goal and *after.* The main objective is achieved by means of reaching subordinate, component objectives, so during dinner preparation or during class, some of these component objectives are achieved. One component objective for the dinner is to obtain all the necessary food. Another is to get the turkey into the oven at the right time. Similarly, in class, students achieve a main objective by means of accomplishing smaller tasks, such as learning vocabulary, comprehending the textbook reading, and staying focused on the writing assignment. These in-class objectives are themselves important, and they can make a beginning teacher feel that classroom activities are filled with objectives—as they certainly are. But the teacher must also keep the bigger, main objectives in mind. Because activities merely serve objectives, they can go awry without changing the outcome. The main objectives can still be reached by other routes. Returning to the Thanksgiving dinner example, if your pumpkin pie burns in the oven, you can pick up another pie from the supermarket and still achieve your main objective of a great shared meal. In the classroom, if your students are not remembering vocabulary definitions after looking up words in a dictionary, you can design a game or a nonverbal way for them to illustrate the meanings of the words they must know. The right activity—the well-chosen activity—is the one that achieves the objective.

Bloom's Taxonomy: A Framework for Objectives

Benjamin Bloom (1956) oversaw the creation of a taxonomy of educational goals in the cognitive domain—a description of the different kinds of thinking that people do and how they use information. Bloom's taxonomy is extremely useful when designing instruction because it provides information about thinking and learning that we can apply to the creation of learning goals. Bloom's idea was that the most basic level of thinking is Knowledge, by which he meant taking in data or facts that could later be listed or recited from memory. The next level is Comprehension, which involves understanding what memorized facts mean. At this level, the learner can explain the facts or concepts in his or her own words. Bloom's higher levels of thinking are Application, Analysis, Synthesis, and Evaluation. Although Bloom's taxonomy has been modified over the years, it remains a bedrock for understanding intellectual work, which makes it invaluable to teachers in their planning, instruction, and assessment.

Instructional designers can find additional guidance for framing objectives in a notable revision of Bloom's taxonomy published in the book *A Taxonomy for Learning, Teaching, and Assessing* (Anderson et al., 2001). As Figure 2.1 shows, the updated hierarchies presented by Lorin W. Anderson and his colleagues replace Bloom's original nouns with verbs and reorganize the highest levels of thinking.

Figure 2.1 • The Original and Revised Version of Bloom's Taxonomy

Bloom's Original Hierarchy of Thinking Skills (1956)	Revision by Anderson et al. (2001)
1. Knowledge	1. Remember
2. Comprehension	2. Understand
3. Application	3. Apply
4. Analysis	4. Analyze
5. Synthesis	5. Evaluate
6. Evaluation	6. Create

Over time, lists of verbs have been generated to clarify what kinds of thinking are associated with each level of Bloom's taxonomy (see Appendix A). Both the taxonomy and these verb lists can be helpful when you are trying to articulate what you want students to be able to do as a result of learning the material in a lesson or unit. Determining how deep and how broad students' learning should be becomes easier when you can consider various possibilities and zero in on those that constitute a level of learning that satisfies you. At the simplest level, for example, you might stipulate that students be able to recite certain facts, such as "Whales and bats are mammals." At intermediate levels, you might want them to be able to organize mammals into categories and compare and contrast the habitats and the living requirements of these animals. To get your students working at the most complex level of thinking—either Synthesis and Evaluation (Bloom, 1956) or Evaluating and Creating (Anderson et al., 2001)—you could require them to study the effects of changes in habitats of certain animals, communicate with various governmental agencies and special-interest groups about the consequences of these changes, and make recommendations for dealing with them. Achieving these objectives would require that students have a broad knowledge of the animals, their habitats, the human activities that affect these habitats, and governmental oversight, among other things. Students would need to pull together information from a variety of disciplines to create a full picture and, after evaluating the information to determine a logical course of action, communicate the results of their work.

Objectives Related to Attitudes and Values

We have defined objectives as "statements of what students will know and be able to do at the end of a lesson." The examples that we have examined are all concerned with students' taking in new information and being able to use it. Benjamin Bloom (1956) organized learning objectives into three domains: cognitive, affective, and psychomotor. The cognitive domain is where most teachers' and students' attention is focused, and it is the domain of academic standards. However, most teachers do have affective goals for their students as well as cognitive, knowledge-building goals. As described by Krathwohl, Bloom, and Masia (1964), affective goals

> emphasize a feeling tone, an emotion, or a degree of acceptance or rejection. Affective objectives vary from simple attention to selected phenomena to complex but internally consistent qualities of character and conscience. We found

a large number of such objectives in the literature expressed as interests, attitudes, appreciations, values, and emotional sets or biases. (p. 7)

These authors stated firmly, "The fact that we attempt to analyze the affective area separately from the cognitive is not intended to suggest that there is a fundamental separation. There is none" (p. 45). The artificial separation of thinking and feeling is done for convenience, and the separation is almost never complete. Krathwohl and his colleagues found that "nearly all cognitive objectives have an affective component if we search for it" (p. 48).

The role of affective goals will, of course, vary according to the subject, the teacher, the students, and the situation. In a private religious school, for example, certain affective goals may be obvious, and their achievement is likely to be a matter of considerable importance. In public schools, affective goals commonly take the form of instilling in students an appreciation of the subject under study. Courses in the arts, including literature, are likely to include affective goals, but so are courses in math, science, social studies, physical education, and everything else. We hope, for example, that students in driver's education will value and want to practice safe driving. It goes without saying that they must know how to drive safely, but our adult expectation that they *recognize the importance* of safe driving practices and choose to employ them is a goal in the affective domain.

To grasp the criticality of affective goals, we have only to imagine a school in which students are successfully achieving all our purely cognitive goals but none of our affective ones. If young people swear at each other, attack each other, lie, cheat, steal, *and* despise intellectual work, no amount of skill at calculus, no amount of historical knowledge, and no creative ability in the arts will compensate for or justify it. Affective goals are essential to raising healthy young people, just as they are essential to the creation and perpetuation of a civil society.

However, as Krathwohl and his colleagues (1964) pointed out, affective goals are difficult to assess, and in our culture we generally consider an individual's attitudes and enthusiasm to be private business. Still, as people who work intensively with young people, teachers will have affective goals for students and will continue to require civil behavior from them. Teachers will continue to do what they can to instill in students an appreciation for the content that they teach:

> The careful observer of the classroom can see that the wise teacher as well as the psychological theorist uses the cognitive behavior and the achievement of cognitive goals to attain affective goals. In many instances she does so more intuitively than consciously. In fact, a large part of what we call "good teaching" is the teacher's ability to attain affective objectives through challenging the students' fixed beliefs and getting them to discuss issues. (Krathwohl et al., 1964, p. 55)

Although their study was limited to educational objectives in secondary and college courses, this observation about teachers' ways of attaining affective goals is certainly applicable to all grade levels. The particular pedagogical techniques will vary, but the strategy of using increased knowledge to achieve desired feelings and attitudes is widespread.

In this book, I concentrate on cognitive objectives. Teachers must recognize the distinction, however artificial, between objectives for intellectual work that result in building knowledge and developing intellectual skills and objectives aimed at shaping students' feelings and interests. Particularly when grading, it is important to be aware of grades that reflect student learning, on one hand, and those that reflect a student's attitude or willingness to cooperate, on the other. As Krathwohl and his colleagues (1964) observed, human beings operate as whole organisms who rarely separate thinking completely from feeling, so affective goals for students can be embedded in what appear to be cognitive goals so long as the cognitive goals are clearly identified and stated.

Let's take another look at the science teacher's trip to the meadow. As a person who loves the natural world and wants students to love it too, the teacher planning this field trip may be thinking, "The revised objectives that focus exclusively on students' knowledge of numbers of species and the ways species interact take all the heart and joy out of exploring a meadow. It limits the meadow experience to list making! These cognitive objectives will leave the students behaving like robots." To increase the chances that the natural world will delight as well as inform students, this teacher may design some introductory activities that encourage open-ended exploration of the meadow's beauty and richness before asking the students to begin listing species. These activities would serve affective goals (Bloom, 1956; Krathwohl et al., 1964), and they are important.

When a teacher or student looks for fun, beauty, awe, horror, or other emotions in an experience, he or she is operating in the affective domain. Because affective goals coexist with cognitive ones, the two types frequently reinforce each other. At least in some cases, the more we appreciate the value of something, the easier it is to focus on it and learn about it. The more we learn about it, the easier it is to appreciate its value. When this is not the case, it may be because the cognitive load placed on learners is too heavy to allow them to develop positive attitudes toward the subject. It may also be because the cognitive demands are not appropriate for the students' developmental level and, therefore, not aligned with their affective states. This can happen, for example, when students are required to learn material that they are unable to connect to their lives and interests.

In the example of the meadow lesson, cognitive instructional objectives are the best way to ensure that students will develop intellectual capital as a result of the wonderful experience of exploring nature. Instructional objectives in the cognitive domain do not describe everything that occurs in a learning activity; they describe just the skills and knowledge that relate to students' learning—to the intellectual work that learners do.

Criticism of Objective-Based Instruction

Two arguments against objective-based instruction arise from a belief that objectives fundamentally limit learning rather than encourage it. Some educators argue that it is impossible to predict the range of ideas and responses that students evince in the course of engagement with a body of knowledge or a work of art. To a person making this argument, establishing objectives feels like shutting down intellectual excursions into new territory—excursions that can lead to surprising and rewarding discoveries for which a teacher might not have thought to create objectives.

A similar argument contends that basing instruction on specific objectives, and then evaluating learning through assessments designed to measure attainment of those objectives, ignores the grander scheme of possible intellectual and cultural attainment. In this view, "objectives" describe mere skill training, and factual data are associated with old educational practices of rote memorization and drill. Someone making this argument might ask, "How can students profitably investigate the big questions of the human condition if they spend all their time memorizing details?"

These criticisms are valid only if we assume two things. The first is that the instructional objectives on the lesson plan are the only learning outcomes available to students during that lesson. In practice, however, a lesson's specific instructional objectives describe a baseline of what every student must end the lesson knowing and being able to do. Objectives never limit what might be learned, and an enthusiastic and knowledgeable teacher brings more information and thought-provoking ideas to a lesson than just those predicted by the instructional objectives. In Chapter 10, we'll explore sample lesson-plan formats you can use to draw connections between instructional objectives and larger issues of human culture and experience so that you can deliberately bring these kinds of "essential questions" (Wiggins & McTighe, 2005) into your classroom.

The second assumption behind this criticism is that objectives describe only the lowest levels of Bloom's taxonomy—those associated with attaining factual knowledge. In fact, Bloom's work was inspired by a desire not only to record what kinds of thinking college students were required to do when taking examinations but also to ensure that the higher levels of thinking were included. If you want your students' learning to be at the higher levels —appreciating the complexity of the natural world, for example, or seeing how human history is told in multiple ways—you can write objectives aimed to target this kind of achievement. After all, the thinking and performance of the great scholars in any field are described by their colleagues in terms of analytical ability, creative synthesis, and insightful evaluation. If their thinking and performance can be so described, so can our students'.

Objectives and Assessment

When writing objectives, it's important to remember that you'll need to design an assessment for each and every one of them.

We will take a close look at assessment in Chapter 7, but it's important to touch on the topic here, in a general discussion of objectives, because assessments are a powerful tool for making objectives stronger. Thinking about how you can assess an objective helps you write it in specific, focused language. If an objective is too vague, it won't tell you how students can demonstrate that they have learned. As you learn how to write objectives and how to assess your students' progress toward achieving them, you will recognize assessments and objectives are two sides of one coin. As we'll see in the next chapter, clearly written objectives contain within them the seeds of good assessment.

3

A Closer Look at the
Language of Objectives

Objectives are statements of what students will know and be able to do after they have learned what we intend for them to learn. This definition requires that teachers setting out to write objectives take a very close look at the changes we want students to make to their existing knowledge. Do we want them to add facts to their knowledge database? See relationships? Correct misunderstandings? Develop nuanced and sophisticated conceptual understandings? This definition of "objectives" also explains why Bloom's taxonomy, in its original and updated forms, is so valuable for teachers writing educational objectives: it helps us understand what forms human thinking takes and guides us toward the appropriate cognitive outcomes of our teaching. The language of objectives, then, is chosen to describe the thinking and learning that students do. We write all objectives to be *student-centered* and *thinking-centered*.

When objectives are written to be both student-centered and thinking-centered, the language will also give essential (if not detailed) information about students' newfound performance capabilities—what they can do as a result of their thinking and learning. In this chapter, we'll look at how careful attention to the language of objectives can bring new clarity to lesson planning and support our ability to achieve desired learning outcomes.

Writing Objectives That Are Student-Centered

Contrast these two objectives:

> *Students will hear a lecture on graphing linear equations.*
>
> *Students will graph linear equations.*

Having read Chapter 2, you'll recognize the first of these objectives as a description of classroom activity rather than of student learning. Although this objective implies that students will learn to graph equations, its primary focus is what the teacher will do. It is possible for this objective to be carried out successfully (that is, for the teacher to deliver the planned lecture) without resulting in much student learning. Note, too, that this objective also reflects the assumption that if students engage in a particular activity (in this case, if they hear a lecture), they will inevitably learn the right things from it (how to graph linear equations).

The second objective, by contrast, describes a true end point of the learning process: what students will do as a result of a lesson on how to graph linear equations. The principal in the hallway probably doesn't want to hear just what happened in class ("We heard a lecture on graphing equations."); that principal is interested in what students have learned—what they are taking with them into the world outside the classroom. What matters most after class is that each student can truthfully say, "I can graph linear equations. Here, I'll show you how it's done."

Focusing on What Students Must Do

A wonderful consequence of writing objectives that are student-centered and thinking-centered is this: *it trains the teacher's attention on students' thinking*. Great teachers pay close attention to their students' intellectual activity. Beginning teachers may be understandably focused primarily on their own teaching behavior, but what really matters is what goes on in the students' minds. Having an established objective for students' intellectual work and the skills that result from that work keeps both teachers and students focused on learning at the required level.

Choosing to define objectives as "descriptions of what students will know and be able to do as a result of their learning" stresses that students need to able to do two things—one internal and one external. The first thing (knowing) is something intellectual and, therefore, internal: students will be able to think in a particular way about certain things. The second (doing) is something observable and, therefore, external: they will be able to use their intellectual gains to perform certain tasks that can be witnessed. One could argue that a simpler definition of objectives would be "descriptions of what students will be able to do," period. After all, thinking is a form of doing, and one of a teacher's tasks is to monitor students' mental activity. However, the conception of objectives as descriptions of what students will know *and* be able to do provides a useful reminder that good objectives address both the internal and external skills.

The key point about the language of valid instructional objectives is that all verbs appropriate for use in instructional objectives describe simultaneously two critically important features of learning: the kind of thinking that students do and, by extension, their ability to use that thinking in a visible performance. Consider the following objective:

> *Students will analyze King's use of figurative language in "I Have a Dream."*

Here, the verb "analyze" describes the kind of thinking students will do (the internal activity) and also describes students' ability to explain how figurative language contributes to the effects of the speech (the external activity). If students have adequately analyzed, they will be able to explain the results of their analysis in some way or medium.

Following the Format

Teachers' responsibility for monitoring student learning is the reason that virtually all formal lesson plans require objectives to take the form of "Students will . . ." followed by a verb that (1) describes the kind of thinking that will be required and (2) gives some information about the kind of performance or skill students are to master. The details of the performance do not have to be spelled out in the objective, as the verbs used convey the general parameters of the students' new skill provide clarification.

For example, a teacher's objective might be

Students will solve long-division problems.

When we consult a chart of Bloom's taxonomy, we see that the verb "solve" means this teacher will be asking students to think and perform at the Application level. To master this objective, they don't have to analyze or evaluate anything; they just need to know how to apply the steps of long division in math problems. In choosing this verb, the teacher is describing a kind of thinking as well as a performance that demonstrates that thinking.

A teacher who wants students to explain why they take the steps that they do while applying the steps of long division will be asking them to think at a higher level—that of Analysis. In that case, the objective should use one of the verbs associated with the Analysis level and might look something like this:

Students will explain the function of each step in solving long-division problems.

A teacher who knows the language of objectives will note the difference in these levels of thinking and will know that the performance required of students reflects the difference. Such a teacher will be able to teach to a targeted outcome and design appropriate assessments.

Bloom's taxonomy assumes that each level of thinking includes all the levels below it. For example, if you ask your students to explain the rationale behind each step of solving a math problem, you're assuming, correctly according to Bloom, that students who can do this can also work at the Application level and solve the problems that they are explaining.

Using the Active Voice

One final requirement for writing student-centered objectives is to use the active voice rather than the passive. Consider these three objectives:

> *Students will be given a handout.*
>
> *Students will be put into groups.*
>
> *Students will get a lesson on using Internet sources.*

On the surface, these may look like student-centered statements. The first word of each is "students"! What these really are, however, are teacher-centered statements disguised by the passive voice. The first, "Students will be given a handout," is a teacher-centered statement about providing a handout. For the focus to be on student learning, this objective must be stated in terms of what students will know and be able to do as a result of using this handout. Once the teacher has pinpointed what learning should result from the handout activity, the objective can be written this way:

> *Students will conjugate "avoir" and "etre."*

The handout—and indeed, any instructional activity a teacher might opt for—is merely the vehicle for students' intellectual work. Don't let an activity distract you from the real goal.

The second of these examples, "Students will be put into groups," is clearly a description of what the teacher will do. Again, to determine what the true objective is, focus on student learning. It could be something like

> *Students will collaborate in groups of three to solve geometry problems.*

In this case, the real goal is to solve the math problems, and the information about group work addresses *how* rather than *what* students will learn. As such, it belongs in the "learning activities" part of the lesson plan (see Chapter 9). Although it is not wrong to include the *how* in an objective, it's not essential to do so. What *is* wrong is omitting the description of the thinking and learning students will do.

The third of these examples, "Students will get a lesson on using Internet sources," is the teacher's perception of what will happen when the class goes to the media center to do some research. If we focus on student learning outcomes, the result will be something like this:

> *Students will use the Internet to locate reliable sources of information about Picasso.*

This objective makes it clear that this lesson is primarily about using the Internet, not learning about Picasso. (Objectives for learning about the artist could be stated separately—something like "Students will describe characteristics of cubism as developed by Picasso and Braque.") This example illustrates another advantage of being clear about the objective of a classroom activity: it prevents a potentially confusing amalgam of goals. In this case, had the teacher not made sure that the students would be focusing on what constitutes reliable sources, they might have assumed that the point of the lesson was to simply find something—anything—about Picasso.

Writing Objectives That Are Thinking-Centered

Which of the following objectives are thinking-centered?

> *Students will visit the Gettysburg museum.*
>
> *Students will include a title page on their reports.*
>
> *Students will learn to love literature.*

Trick question! The answer is none. Although all three are associated to some degree with students' thinking, none of them clearly states what kind of thinking students will do. None states a cognitive learning outcome. Students who visit the museum may or may not engage intellectually with the exhibits. The students who comply with the teacher's requirements for formatting reports are, at best, learning what a title page is, but they are not making progress toward mastering academic standards. And "Students will learn to love literature," the third objective in this list, describes feeling rather than thinking, and so properly belongs in the affective domain rather than the cognitive domain. (More information about objectives in the affective domain can be found in Goleman, 1995; Krathwohl, Bloom, & Masia, 1964; and Noddings, 1984.)

What Is Thinking?

A closer examination of the connection between stated objectives and student thinking requires that we consider what we mean by "thinking" and "intellectual work" (synonyms in this context).

Our brains are capable of many kinds of activity, only some of which are cognitive. A useful definition of thinking for teachers and learners comes from the website Biology Online (n.d.), where thinking is described as "mental activity, not predominantly perceptual, by which one apprehends some aspect of an object or situation based on past learning and experience." This definition emphasizes apprehension and connection to existing knowledge, leading us to consider other kinds of cognitive activity that may be precursors to apprehending, such as considering, exploring, and wondering. These cognitive activities may be part of a learning process but would be appropriate as learning outcomes only if you were teaching students how to consider, explore, or wonder; if you were doing that, you would be teaching them *how to learn* rather than teaching them the content of academic standards. Although thinking may be unconscious—such as when we sleep on a decision or wonder idly about something and then experience a flash of insight—most school learning involves conscious thinking that engages the learner's forebrain and requires the active connection of new information to existing knowledge. Thinking is also associated with emotions and social interaction, which often help the learner engage in intellectual work, but in this discussion of objectives, we will focus on cognition.

Objectives Describe and Require Thinking

In the cognitive domain, all true instructional objectives describe a thinking process. Remembering, reasoning, and creating are all types of thinking, as are the other mental processes included in Bloom's taxonomy, such as applying, analyzing, and synthesizing. If a learner remembers information that he or she has taken in and uses it to answer a factual question, that learner is thinking on the most basic level of "knowledge." If the learner uses new (and old) information to solve a problem, create a product, draw conclusions, or evaluate a situation, that learner is thinking on one of the higher levels.

For example, a student who can find images in a poem is using knowledge about a type of literary device and applying it to the problem or situation at hand. In short, the student is doing intellectual work that can be described by this objective:

Students will identify images in a poem.

And if the student writes a poem using images, that work can be described by this objective:

Students will create a poem that includes imagery.

Remember, all the verbs used in objectives describe some kind of intellectual work. The higher-level thinking skills, such as those at the Synthesis, Evaluation, and Creation levels, require the most sophisticated and wide-ranging mental effort, but all levels of thinking may be represented in the language of instructional objectives. Even those activities at the lowest end of Bloom's taxonomy, such as reciting or listing from memory, require some mental work, as does every performance that demonstrates learning. Bloom's taxonomy also reminds us that these "lower levels" of thinking are a necessary foundation for the higher levels.

Another key point about Bloom's taxonomy that instructional designers should know is that the so-called lower levels of thinking and learning are not necessarily the easiest, nor are higher levels the most difficult. Each level can be experienced in a way that challenges the learner, and each may be experienced as relatively easy. The first level of Knowledge/Remembering is difficult if it requires memorizing long passages of Latinate prose or elaborate mathematical formulas, or if a particular student has trouble memorizing. The highest level of Evaluation/Creating can be stress-free if the student is well-prepared and inspired to carry out the assigned task.

Choosing the most accurate language for objectives is a matter of thinking carefully about how best to describe the desired learning outcomes. Because instructional designers must pinpoint the different kinds of learning outcomes they want to pursue, selecting one verb over another usually indicates significant differences in the instruction they plan to deliver and the kind of thinking and performance they expect of their students.

Instructional Objectives Describe What Students Will Learn to *Do*

Well-designed instructional objectives do more than just state what kind of thinking and learning should occur; they also go far toward establishing what kind of task or performance the students will do to demonstrate their learning. A particular level of thinking and learning will allow students to do a particular kind of demonstration of that thinking and learning. We can use Bloom's taxonomy both to understand what intellectual work and performances we are requiring of our students and to describe our requirements in clear language.

For example, if you decide that you want your students to be able to recite a famous speech, you can state your objective in that straightforward way:

Students will recite a famous speech from memory.

You will be asking them to engage in the Knowledge (Bloom, 1956) or Remembering (Anderson et al., 2001) level of learning. To demonstrate achievement of this objective, a student needs to orally deliver an accurate reproduction of the chosen speech. If you want students to recite the famous speech and understand what it means, you will be asking for the next higher level of learning, Comprehension (Bloom) or Understanding (Anderson et al.), and you'll need to create additional objectives to clarify what about the speech you want students to understand. You might say

Students will paraphrase the speech in their own words
or

Students will explain the historical references in the speech
or
Students will summarize the conflicts described in the speech.

You might tie the oral delivery to Comprehension:

Students will recite a speech from memory using voice and body to express interpretation.

And if you want students to compare and contrast this speech with something else, or to interpret deeper meaning, you will be requiring a still higher level of thinking—the level of Analysis.

At all levels, it is essential to understand the link between intellectual work and performance, lest you expect students to demonstrate a level of learning that's beyond the actual learning set out in the objective. For example, if you tell students to read an essay about the Kennedy administration, they are likely to be looking for information that they can recite back to you—that is, they are likely to be operating at the two most basic levels of thinking and learning—Knowledge and Comprehension. If you expect students to explain the long-term consequences of some of Kennedy's decisions, which will call for higher levels of thinking, such as Analysis and Synthesis, many of them will not be able to do so without repeated closer readings of the essay and further guidance in interpreting what they have read. If they understand from the start what kind of thinking and subsequent performance you expect, they will know what kind of reading they need to do and what questions to ask, increasing the odds that they will achieve your objectives.

A Phrase That Sums Up Useful Instructional Objectives: "Show Me!"

Clear instructional objectives state what the learner is expected to *do* both intellectually and as a physical demonstration of that intellectual work, and this is the main reasons why instructional objectives are also known as "performance objectives." Whatever form the performance takes, it provides an opportunity for students to show how they can use their thinking and their learning. Wiggins and McTighe's (2005) *Understanding by Design* provides a thorough discussion of the many types of performances that can demonstrate understanding.

Keeping the students' performances in mind can help you write strong objectives. When you're wondering if your objective is clear and specific enough, ask yourself if you can visualize the students doing what the objective says they will do. Although visualizing students in action is not a foolproof test of a good objective, because it is possible to visualize students engaged in learning activities just as easily, visualizing is a good way to transform a general goal into a specific instructional objective.

For example, if you begin planning by thinking that you want your students to know how to divide fractions, try visualizing a student who has successfully completed your lessons and who now *does* understand division of fractions. How will you know that this student understands? What problems can this student solve? What can this student answer questions about, explain, or describe? What will this student say to the superintendent in the hallway who asks, "What can you do now that you couldn't do before?" If your instructional objectives state that

> *Students will solve problems of dividing fractions*

> and

> *Students will apply knowledge of dividing fractions to real-world situations*

the successful student will be able to tell the superintendent, "I can divide fractions. I can do it on paper, and I can do it with real things. If you give me half a pizza, I can divide it up among five people so that everybody gets a tenth of a whole pizza."

When in doubt about whether your instructional objectives are specific and concrete enough, try using Robert Mager's (1984) visualization-based Hey Dad test, which involves imagining the aspects of the learning a successful student would be able to show off to Dad, Mom, or anyone else. Experiment with phrasing your objective so that your students can say something like

- "Hey, Dad! Come watch me _____ !"
- "Hey, Mom! Wanna hear me _____ ?"
- "Hey, Grandma! Look at this _____ I made!"

Suppose you begin your planning with this:

> *Students will understand the basic concept of metaphor.*

It may be a good general goal, but it is a poor instructional objective, and that's because we have to guess what the students will be able to do as a result of understanding the concept of metaphors. A student can't very well say, "Hey, Dad! Watch me understand the basic concept of metaphors!"

With this phrasing, we don't know how deep an understanding of metaphor students are required to have or what forms that understanding might take. But you can take a step toward a much better objective by asking, "What might students do to convince me that they understand metaphor? When I visualize a successful learner, what do I see?"

You might start by thinking about the foundation of students' understanding, which is usually simply the ability to *identify* or *define* something. Do you want students to be able to tell you what a metaphor is and be able to identify metaphors in text? You might want students to proceed beyond this to the next level of understanding—being able to *explain* why an author may have used a certain metaphor. You might also want students to *select* a good metaphor for a certain purpose from a list of possibilities, or to *create* a metaphor of their own. Although you cannot directly watch students "understand," you can directly watch (or hear) them identify, define, explain, select, and create. And these explicit performances would be acceptable evidence of understanding:

- "Hey, Dad! Come see how I can identify metaphors in this poem!"
- "Hey, Mom! Wanna hear me define metaphor?"
- "Hey, Grandma! Listen to this great metaphor I came up with!"

Students' actions—what they can do with their knowledge—is the link between objectives and assessments. Instructional objectives and the assessments that are aligned with them describe two halves of a single process. Chapter 7 addresses assessments in detail, but here it is important to note that in choosing language that expresses objectives accurately, we are also choosing language that expresses important information about the assessment.

Objectives tell us what level of intellectual work students are doing and thereby determine what demonstrations of skill they are prepared to do. Imagine, for example, that we state the following as our objective:

*Students will describe characters in "The Fisherman
and His Wife"*

We know that the assessment will specify a way for students to describe characters and, in doing so, will articulate the way that students will use the intellectual work that they have done in comprehending that aspect of the story. They might describe characters orally or in writing; in groups or alone; on a poster; in a booklet; or through music, drawing, skits, or tableaux. It is not necessary to be specific about the form that an assessment takes when writing an objective, but when deciding what assessment to use, the instructional designer benefits from operating within the parameters that a well-written objective provides.

Transforming the Language of Objectives from Colloquial to Professional

We have been examining what it means for objectives to be centered on students' thinking and their demonstration of intellectual skills. This examination shows us that moving from colloquial to professional language in objectives is almost always a matter of tightening the focus to describe more precisely what students will know and be able to do as a result of instruction. This process can be difficult at first, but with practice in thinking about your students' learning and clarifying for yourself what they need to be able to do, you will find these professional statements of your instructional objectives come more and more easily.

The natural language with which instructional designers begin the process of writing objectives—using verbs such as "learn" or "study"—is excellent for brainstorming the content of a lesson or unit but is too general to serve good objectives. These verbs don't describe the extent of learning, the type of thinking, or the students' demonstration of learning. For example, if the objective states, "Students will learn what services the government provides," we still need to know what students are supposed to learn about these services. Will they be able to identify these government services from a list of possibilities? Describe them generally in terms of protecting the population and supporting the economy? Explain those services they personally benefit from? Organize the services according to the level of government that provides them? "Learn" is too general a term to be useful in describing the new knowledge students should have.

"Understand" is another commonly used example of a general goal of instruction. Other common general goals of instruction are "know," "explore," and "be familiar with" a topic. These are all statements about what, presumably, will be in the student's mind, but none of these verbs states clear instructional objectives, because there are so many levels of understanding and so many ways of knowing, being familiar with, or exploring something that we need to specify how broad or deep the understanding or learning must be. Students, too, must be guided to the required level of learning so that they don't assume they should be working with academic content at a level different from the one the teacher expects.

Using Bloom's taxonomy to select the desired kinds of thinking, learning, and performing helps instructional designers keep students' thinking at the forefront of the planning process. Eventually, planning for student learning (rather than for the teacher's performance) will become automatic, and consulting verb charts will no longer be necessary. For now, let us consider some verbs that are often used in objectives—some successfully and some not.

Examples of words or phrases that are too general or open to interpretation to be useful as instructional objectives include the following:

understand	know	explore	learn
comprehend	be exposed to	get a sense of	see
appreciate	be familiar with	think about	realize

All of these are commonsense terms that any teacher might use in the early stages of designing instruction when deciding what students should learn in a lesson or unit or semester. Once you have selected content using these terms, you can develop solid instructional objectives from your general goals. One way to do this is to experiment with words that describe levels of thinking and visible or audible performances, such as

list	define	describe	summarize
identify	explain	compare	diagram
rephrase	draw	contrast	design
tell	solve	create	evaluate

Try visualizing your students using their new content knowledge for the thinking and actions that these verbs describe. Some require only memorization of facts; others require much more complex intellectual work. As you experiment with the verbs in the above list, consider which ones capture the kinds and levels of learning that you deem important. Also keep in mind that the smaller the scope of the lesson, the more specific the content must be in the statement of your objective. For example, if your general goal is that students understand the causes of the French Revolution, you might create objectives like these:

> *Students will describe challenges to the "Old Regime" made by peasants, the bourgeoisie, and aristocrats*

and

> *Students will explain how challenges to the "Old Regime" contributed to the start of the Revolution.*

These instructional objectives show clearly two things students must master on their way to achieving a general goal of "understanding the causes of the French Revolution." But if this content is too broad to be covered in a single lesson, you might narrow your objective, like this:

> *Students will explain the nature and purposes of the "books of grievances" created in preparation for the Estates-General of 1789.*

Let's pause here to see how different this objective would be if we replaced the verb "explain" with a verb that does not describe what knowledge students will gain and what they will do with that knowledge:

> *Students will explore the nature and purposes of the "books of grievances" created in preparation for the Estates-General of 1789.*

When students *explore* a topic, they may learn a great deal, or they may learn virtually nothing. They may learn what we want them to learn, or they may learn facts that we consider trivial. The mistake in using "explore" is a familiar one—the assumption that if students go through an experience, they will learn what they are supposed to learn. However, if we imagine a student telling Mom and Dad that the class poked around the Internet exploring the French Revolution, we have a very different picture from that of a student explaining the nature and purposes of the books of grievances.

As you design daily instruction, you will certainly need to focus on specific content points, such as the books of grievances. But the content points you select will always be part of larger instructional goals for broader content areas, and the objectives that you write for units and for daily work will reflect their different design purposes. For example, if your larger goals for the unit on the French Revolution include getting students to understand the historical context of that event, you will want them to pull together knowledge of the French Revolution and knowledge of the Enlightenment and the Napoleonic Wars, among other things. As their understanding of these events broadens and fills out with details, they will understand (if you decide they should) how the French Revolution affected other nations and the development of modern France. For these broader unit goals, your objectives will provide less specific content data, as illustrated here:

Students will analyze, in the context of the French Revolution, various social, political, economic, and military events in 18th and 19th century France.

Students will design a display that presents the causes, events, and consequences of the French Revolution.

Keep in mind that although the content addressed by objectives will vary according to breadth of study (they may be written for anything from a yearlong course to a 10-minute lesson), any and all levels of thinking might be appropriate at any point. It is more common for unit goals to require higher levels of intellectual work, but unit goals may also require lower levels of learning, particularly when they relate to content that you might want to introduce to students but that they do not need to remember in great detail. Similarly, if you are teaching a lesson focused on a small but essential content point, you may well require students to analyze, synthesize, and evaluate.

There will come a time, probably toward the end of a unit, when you want your students to address a large body of content in a single lesson. This usually requires students to make connections, to synthesize by drawing on a variety of sources, and perhaps to create something new (to them) out of all the elements they have been studying. The work done that day may seem to violate the rule of smaller content for individual lessons. But what is actually happening is that the amount of *new* content is small. In this context, students are referring to what they have learned in the past, so they are not dealing with a large amount of new content. Although the topic is broad and learners' thinking must be broad, the new content—relationships between known entities—is relatively limited.

Examine the Context of the Verbs You Choose

Sometimes it is tempting to take a shortcut and select a verb from one of the many collections of verbs derived from Bloom's taxonomy without taking time to seriously consider its implications for students' learning. This gives the illusion of speeding up the planning process, but is likely to result in trouble later on, during instruction and assessment. The verbs selected from a list may fail to accurately express the intellectual work that students should do. Furthermore, this shortcut can be confusing to both the teacher and the students, because some verbs describe thinking and a performance in some contexts but not others. Let's take a closer look at this phenomenon and the key verbs involved.

"Recognize"

Consider this statement:

> *Students will recognize the chemical elements in a list of elements and compounds.*

In this objective, "recognize" is synonymous with "identify," which is an acceptable verb for an objective. However, it's possible to read "recognize" in a general way that can leave you guessing what students will be able to do at the end of the lesson:

> *Students will recognize the importance of the periodic table.*

Put yourself in the school hallway, interviewing students as they emerge from this lesson. If they say, "I recognize the importance of the periodic table," you might wonder how meaningful that recognition is and what it enables the student to do. The objective as written does not guide the assessor or the student toward passing the Hey Dad test ("Watch me recognize the importance of ___!"). That's because this objective is primarily in the affective domain, focused more on value than on knowledge.

To improve this objective by placing it squarely in the cognitive domain, visualize a student who recognizes the importance of the periodic table. Imagine what he or she can do with the knowledge that this objective hints at. Then state precisely what you see that student doing. First, perhaps

Students will use the periodic table to make predictions about properties of elements

and then

Students will explain the arrangement of elements into groups and periods in the periodic table.

These more specific objectives show that the teacher is thinking about the intellectual work that students do as they learn to read and use the periodic table. This intellectual work can be demonstrated in ways that settle any doubts about what students know and are able to do.

"Apply" and "Use"

These two verbs also may refer to performance in some contexts but not all. Consider this objective:

Students will design a simple experiment, applying [or using] *observation, hypothesis testing, and prediction.*

It clearly describes students' learning and ability. They cannot do the work stated in this objective without thinking and knowing. However, if the context of "apply" or "use" is too general or too subjective, the objective will not be useful. For example, imagine a 5th grade teacher who wants her students to apply their real-world experiences to a science lesson. Possible objectives might look like this:

Students will apply personal experience to explaining static electricity

or

Students will use their personal experiences to understand static electricity.

When we think about the real goal of teaching (student learning) and the purpose of objectives (to state what students will know and be able to do at the end of the lesson), we can see that neither of these two objectives fulfills those purposes very well. The first one may slip under the wire through the use of "explain," although the emphasis in this objective seems to be on the personal experience rather than on the explanation. However, we can imagine a student telling Dad or the principal, "I can explain static electricity using my personal experience," and then going on to deliver an acceptable explanation. But this objective would describe the learning outcome more directly if it focused exclusively on the student's achievement:

Students will explain how static electricity is generated.

If the student chooses to include a personal encounter with static electricity in the explanation, that's fine, but the personal experience doesn't need to be included in the objective. The second objective also emphasizes personal experience and, this time, uses a verb ("understand") that is clearly too broad to be useful.

The real problem with both of these statements of student learning is that they are fundamentally descriptions of learning activities, not of learning objectives. Applying personal experience may be a helpful way to understand and remember the laws of physics related to static electricity, but it is a *way* of learning rather than the learning itself. It is possible to use personal experience and still not be able to explain or apply the relevant facts and concepts related to electrons in motion. If a student tells the principal in the hallway that all she knows is, "When I make my shoes rub against the carpet, I can give my sister a shock," she is not demonstrating that she has done the expected intellectual work in this lesson.

The way for the teacher to untangle these statements' confusing blend of learning activity and objective is to temporarily set aside concerns with *how* the students will learn and concentrate instead on *what* the students will learn: the learning outcome. With the application of personal experiences with electricity reserved for the design of learning activities, the objective of being able to explain and apply knowledge of static electricity can be stated clearly. This approach has the added advantage of putting students who cannot remember personal experiences with static electricity on an equal footing with those who can.

"Imagine"

Being able to imagine is an extremely important intellectual skill; virtually all creative work requires it. Discoveries and inventions are almost always preceded by the discoverer or inventor imagining what might be true or made real—about DNA, about relativity, about music or human behavior . . . the list is endless. Because the process of understanding new knowledge often requires imagining, imagination is a general intellectual skill that all learners need to develop and use when they are learning anything that cannot be experienced directly.

It's true that we need imagination to understand historical events, mathematical concepts, scientific phenomena, fiction, other cultures, and the arts, but in a lesson plan, a focus on imagining belongs in learning activities rather than in statements of instructional objectives. "Imagine" does not work well as a verb in instructional objectives. We cannot see into another person's imagination, and when we ask what a successful student can do with imagining, we find that imagining is not really the desired final outcome. What we really want is thinking and performance that are a result of imagining and are described by more specific verbs that provide more information.

For example, if we ask students to imagine what will happen when glaciers melt, we are asking them to *predict*. If we ask them to imagine another ending to a story, we are asking them to *create* a new ending. If we ask them to imagine another outcome to a war or a court case, we are asking them to *synthesize* knowledge about the societies and people involved and to *construct* a plausible new history based on that knowledge. If *imagining* is really the desired outcome, we would be satisfied with a student telling the principal, "I imagined flying to Jupiter" or "I imagined that I was a porpoise." A student could *imagine* these things without knowing much of anything about Jupiter or porpoises (although the student who did know about them would have a different mental experience from one who did not). These objectives are not really thinking-centered in the way that we are using the term, and they do not pass the Hey Dad test. Whatever cognitive growth might take place during these imaginings is not expressed by the objective.

"Explain" and "Describe"

These two verbs appear quite often in lessons plans, which is understandable, given how often we want students to be able to explain or describe processes, concepts, events, and so on.

Although on charts of Bloom's taxonomy "explain" and "describe" are usually associated with lower levels of thinking, they have a legitimate place in lesson plans where higher levels of thinking are expected, and explaining and describing can both involve quite sophisticated intellectual work. It all depends on the context. For example, students may explain or describe something simple, such as the setting of *Where the Red Fern Grows* (the Ozarks in the early 20th century). On the other hand, they may explain or describe a complex phenomenon that requires mastery of a great deal of information and subsequent intellectual work with it, as in

> *Students will describe the influence of the ancient Greeks on European civilization in the Renaissance.*

The six verbs that we have examined in this section describe intellectual work but require contextual consideration. In reality, all verbs in objectives need to be considered carefully. The critical question to apply to them is "How well does this verb describe the thinking I expect students to do?" The next three chapters provide guidance on how to answer.

4

Two Special Cases When Creating Objectives: *Read* and *Write*

Reading and writing are the foundations of formal education. In the course of their schooling, students will need to learn how to interpret multiple symbol systems and use them to read and generate "texts" of many kinds. Whether you are teaching students to use alphabetic text in the usual sense of reading and writing or working with mathematical, scientific, musical, oral, or visual text, you will almost certainly be incorporating some versions of reading and writing into your instruction and assessment. In this chapter, we will use alphabetic text as the default version for examples of objectives and learning outcomes, but the discussion applies to reading and writing of any kind.

Objectives Involving Reading

What learning outcome does this objective articulate?

Students will read "The Lottery."

The realistic answer is "none." There is no specific learning outcome stated; what students know and can do after they read the story depends on how they read it. Students may gather information, comprehend it, apply previously learned information, analyze, synthesize, or evaluate as they read. Or they may do none of these things. Their reading experience may be almost completely affective (just to enjoy) or completely empty, with the only outcome being the student's belief that he or she read the text but didn't understand or remember any of it.

Because we want our students to be reading—and it is, after all, a cognitive activity—"read" is commonly used as the verb in instructional objectives. An important learning outcome of schooling is that students be able to read productively and comfortably. However, it is significant that Bloom's taxonomy does not include "read"; any and all kinds of thinking may be involved in reading—thinking that's complex and multilayered or concrete and limited. Reading is carried out by individual readers in different ways as they read different kinds of text. As a verb, "read" is as open to interpretation as "know" and equally vague about results. If we state the objective of a lesson or assignment as "Students will read" a particular text, the objective has been met if students read that text in any way. Of course we do not want our students to tell the principal at the end of the lesson, "Yes, I read it, but it was confusing and I didn't understand it." What's necessary to determine is what degree of comprehension—and comprehension of what—we require.

Identify Learning Outcomes

Whenever we assign reading, we must know what we expect students to take from the experience. As an instructional designer, your first step is to decide whether the purpose of a reading assignment is to promote more effective reading, to provide access to content information, or both. Another way to phrase this decision is to ask, "Do I want students to *learn to read,* to *read to learn,* or both?" Whatever way you answer that question, comprehension will probably be one of your desired outcomes, so ask yourself, "What about this text or its content do I want students to comprehend?" As you draft your objectives for the assignment, in the place where you might have used the verb "read" to describe what students will do, try substituting a more specific description of the student learning you want to see:

> *Students will summarize the plot, describe the characters, and analyze the structure of "The Lottery."*

If the lesson really is about reading with fluency and comprehension, reading for vocabulary development, or reading for analysis of genre characteristics, state these outcomes in your objectives:

> *Students will read "The Lottery" aloud* [or silently] *with fluency and comprehension*

or

> *Students will use context clues, analysis of word roots, and the dictionary to define selected words in "The Lottery"*

or

> *Students will identify exposition, rising action, and climax in "The Lottery."*

Likewise, if one of your desired learning outcomes is for students to use reading strategies to make meaning from the text, that's something you can emphasize:

> *Students will use textual clues, questioning, note taking, and collaboration to read "The Lottery."*

Keep in mind that objectives work together to describe the learning you want for your students; no single objective has to stand alone. Put all these objectives about reading "The Lottery" together, and you'll be teaching techniques for improving comprehension and fluency as well as specific information about the story.

If we examine all the objectives we've looked at in this chapter so far to see if they are student-centered, thinking-centered, and performance-centered, they look pretty good. Even "Students will read 'The Lottery'" seems all right—that is, until we visualize different readers telling us what achieving that objective (having read the story) has enabled them to do. Yes, at first glance, this objective appears to pass the Hey Dad test of performance ("Hey Dad, come hear me read this story!"); however, a student might be able to decode the words and read them aloud without gaining an intellectual understanding the story.

Successful reading is a complex task—involving the application of a number of decoding strategies and consideration of various kinds of literary techniques. When we want our students to work at the more complicated end of the reading spectrum, applying the Hey Dad test requires us to do more extensive visualizing—to think of a student and parent sitting down together to examine a text in careful detail. But we certainly can imagine a student saying, "Want to hear how I figured out what's really going on in this weird story? I can show you the clues the author gives us!" Successful learners will indeed be able to explain and demonstrate how they use the strategies that you have taught, just as they will be able to describe characters, summarize plot, and analyze story structure.

Learning About Specific Texts

When creating objectives for lessons that include reading, another question to ask yourself is this: "As long as students know what I want them to know about the subject of this text, does it matter how they get that information?"

If it *doesn't* matter, clearly you are using the text as a source of information that could be replaced by another, with no damage done to your students' learning outcomes. In these cases, reading is the equivalent of watching an informational video or listening to a lecture. In your objective, state what students will know and be able to do as a result of reading, watching, or listening. Avoid saying that they will "read," "watch," or "listen."

When the purpose of the assignment is for students to take in new content, reading, watching, or listening are learning activities, not outcomes.

In situations when it *is* important for students to experience a particular text, ask yourself what you want students to get from that text beyond factual content. For example, does it matter whether your students read the Declaration of Independence itself, or would reading a summary of it written in contemporary language help you achieve the same instructional goal? What is your real purpose in asking students to read texts that they find difficult or boring—like the Declaration of Independence—or Shakespeare, poetry, other original historical documents, or professional scientific writing? It's likely your answer to these questions will touch on a variety of affective and cognitive aims related to aesthetics or to helping students acquire deeper insight into events, people, or concepts.

For example, one significant reason we want our students to read original historical texts is so that they can expand their horizons by experiencing others' language, lives, and ways of thinking. However, "experiencing," as a learning outcome, definitely does not pass the Hey Dad test. A goal like this is an inseparable mixture of cognitive and affective apprehension, reminding us that there is no natural separation of the cognitive and affective domains (Krathwohl et al., 1964). Fortunately, Krathwohl and colleagues provided insight into how cognitive work can foster affective gains. So, in the case of a study of Declaration of Independence, you might express your objectives in this way:

> *Students will summarize the content of the Declaration*
> *of Independence*
>
> or
>
> *Students will describe the effects of the language of the*
> *Declaration of Independence by contrasting Jefferson's rhetoric*
> *with the language of their summaries*
> or

> *Students will analyze the connotations of selected words and phrases in the Declaration of Independence.*

It is not a foregone conclusion that these lessons will lead to the achievement of your affective goals—that every student will admire and take pleasure in the nuances of Jefferson's language. However, the process of exploring Jefferson's rhetorical choices in the light of his purposes and the cultural moment in which he made those choices increases the odds that students will come to respect his literary accomplishment. If you add to the mix your own admiration and appreciation of Jefferson's language as a model of responsive reading, the chances are that much greater.

As another example, consider what kinds of objectives are best suited for challenging literary or historical works, such as Jonathan Swift's "A Modest Proposal." This piece was written in 1729, so much of its language and many of its references are unfamiliar to contemporary readers. Furthermore, it is a satire intended to shock and amuse as well as to provoke and persuade. In short, because adolescents in the 21st century may be baffled by both the content and rhetoric of "A Modest Proposal," a teacher creating objectives for the study of this text must do much more than state that students will read it. Here are some examples of relevant objectives:

> *Students will explain Swift's "proposal" and the reasons he offers for making it.*
>
> *Students will describe the political, economic, and religious conflicts that Swift alludes to.*
>
> *Students will identify passages in which Swift reveals the true state of Ireland's oppression by England.*
>
> *Students will explain the purpose of the final paragraph.*
>
> *Students will analyze the effect of the words and phrases Swift uses to describe Irish people.*

Students will create a description of wealthy people from information that Swift provides.

Students will analyze the role of economics in Swift's depiction of relations between England and Ireland.

Students will evaluate Swift's use of irony.

Students will define "satire" based on this example.

Students will generate "modest proposals" to address contemporary social problems.

You might begin planning by saying, "I want students to read Swift's pamphlet. I want them to appreciate his outrageous ideas and admire his skill. I want them to know how bad social conditions can be for people who are oppressed and to see one way of responding to that oppression." Translating this beginning statement into usable objectives guides you to design learning activities that will

- Prepare students for reading.
- Help them comprehend the text during reading.
- Allow them to work productively and creatively with the text after reading.

It is neither necessary nor advisable to spell out objectives for every single possible element of a complex text. After you have generated a list of possible learning outcomes, select the ones you believe are most important for every student to achieve. Keep in mind that when you choose objectives, you are making a commitment to spend enough class time on them for students to achieve them. These are the objectives you will assess. Additional ideas, background knowledge, interpretations, and insights will come up in discussion and other activities, and they will likely add greatly to the students' understanding, but not everything that happens in a classroom can or needs to be set into an objective.

Brainstorming a list of objectives like the one created for "A Modest Proposal" is a reminder of how much can be done instructionally with a complex text and calls attention to the need to be selective and focused when teaching a text with the potential to take readers in many directions. With complex texts, it's likely your student readers *will* go in many directions and that they'll benefit greatly from their excursions. However, having ensured your objectives describe the outcomes that are most important and that will be assessed, you can be confident in your students' achievement. Those objectives, and the instruction and assessment you've aligned with them, are the best insurance you have that no one will leave your class saying, "That was a dumb story. I didn't understand any of it."

Other particular kinds of texts that we want our students to read include textbooks, newspaper articles, graphical displays, and reports. Learning to read these sources of information opens the door to success in school and continued lifelong learning.

When you establish objectives for these kinds of texts, it is not enough to say, "Students will read Chapter 4 in their textbook" or "Students will read charts" or "Students will read newspaper articles." None of these is a statement of what students will know or be able to do at the end of the lesson. Here are some examples of objectives that describe successful reading of informational texts:

> *Students will use textbook features such as sidebars, glossaries, illustrations, section headings, and review questions to identify, integrate, and explain information about vectors.* (Note: Additional objectives would reveal what students need to know about vectors. This objective states what students will learn about using textbooks.)
>
> *Students will compare and contrast graphically displayed information about Jupiter's moons.*

After reading a newspaper article about a local event, students
will explain who was involved, what happened, and when,
where, and why the event occurred.

A broad definition of reading is "making meaning from text." Objectives for reading are necessary for establishing the extent and kind of meaning that you want your students to make from texts you assign.

Objectives Involving Writing

Take a look at this objective to determine its learning outcomes:

Students will write a two-page research report on a farm animal
of their choice.

The verb "write," like the verb "read," is common in objectives, and there are many reasons why. Writing is a useful way for students to learn; through writing, students can record progress, opinions, and experiences and explore ideas. Writing is also a natural form of assessment, suited for demonstrating all kinds of knowledge in a wide variety of formats. A written research report or essay is a frequent choice for a unit assessment because it requires students to pull together several areas of knowledge and apply a number of different skills.

As an objective, "Students will write a two-page research report on a farm animal of their choice" may appear acceptable at first glance. It is student-centered, it requires thinking, and it does describe a performance. But "write" doesn't tell us what we expect students to learn from the activity of writing. Writing is the *medium* in which students will demonstrate two pages worth of research-based learning about a farm animal, but we can't tell from this objective what that learning ought to comprise. As is true of objectives concerned with reading, objectives that address writing must be analyzed so that the expected results are clear to both teacher and students.

Just as teachers planning a reading assignment must ask whether that assignment's purpose is reading for its own sake or access to content, those planning writing assignments also must consider a number of questions related to purpose: "Is this assignment about learning to write or about demonstrating content knowledge? Is it about exploring a topic through freewriting? Is it about expressing personal experiences and speculations in journals? Or is it about communicating with an audience outside the classroom?"

Because writing comes in so many forms and is useful for many purposes, students as well as teachers must be clear about those purposes; where purposes might overlap; and the implications for audience, assessment, and grading.

Formal Writing Assignments

Formal writing, including the writing of research reports, requires at least three different activities, each of which merits its own objective:

- Conducting the research: gathering, generating, and selecting information
- Learning the topic (you decide what students should know about their topic)
- Drafting, revising, and editing the writing

If the student tells the principal in the hallway, "I wrote a research report on bulls, and here it is," that report might be two pages long, and it might be about bulls, meaning the objective will be met. But the report might also be as much about bullfighting as about bulls on farms, and it might be only marginally comprehensible. The teacher and the student both need to know which parts of the researching, information processing, and writing the student has mastered and which parts need more instruction and practice. Having clear objectives makes this easier for the teacher to manage and for the student to accomplish.

Here's an example. If you expect your students' research reports to include a description of their chosen farm animal *and* an explanation of how the animal is raised and used, that knowledge is part of the desired outcome. Focus on student learning results in this objective:

> *In a two-page research report, students will describe a farm animal, tell how it lives on the farm, and explain what it is used for.*

The writing will need its own objective:

> *Students will write a two-page research report in standard English that includes an introduction, well-organized information, and a conclusion.*

Although before teaching a lesson or making an assignment a teacher must decide what specific skills and knowledge students should achieve, it's not necessary to state all these details in the form of an objective. Component objectives for writing assignments may be expressed in the grading rubric (see Chapter 8). The completeness and accuracy of content could be addressed in the rubric, as could the writer's command of standard written English and composition structures. Writing is like reading in that both are multifaceted processes drawing on a range of skills and knowledge. Neither is limited to a particular kind of thinking: both can require elemental and sophisticated thinking, which is why objectives should always state what kind of thinking and skills students will demonstrate when they read and write. If that information is not stated in instructional objectives, it should be stated in rubrics, assignment descriptions, or grading checklists.

Compare the following "early drafts" of writing-related objectives with their more developed versions:

☒   *Students will write an essay about* Macbeth.

☑ *Students will analyze the theme of what it means to be a man in* Macbeth *in a formal, five-page essay. (Students may choose another theme for analysis.)*

☒ *Students will write in their journals.*

☑ *In journals, students will record their responses to the reading assignment of the previous day, including opinions, questions, associations, and predictions.*

☒ *Students will write a story about a child their age living in Colonial New England.*

☑ *Students will write a story about a child their age living in Colonial New England that includes at least two characters, dialogue, a conflict, and a resolution.*

Students do need to learn how to write independently in a variety of ways and for a range of purposes, so excessively detailed requirements should not be imposed unnecessarily. But until they have enough experience and feedback to be competent writing in journals, creating stories and poems, writing essays and letters, producing research and lab reports, or creating any other specific kind written work, they need comprehensive guidance from the expert who will evaluate their work—their teacher.

Open-Ended Writing Assignments

We have been focusing on objectives that explain what skills and knowledge students should demonstrate in a writing assignment, but you may also want to design writing assignments that are intended to

- Develop students' ability to work independently.
- Allow students to choose the writing they want to do.
- Show you what they have learned from the study of a novel or some other body of knowledge and how they express that learning.

If this is the case, you may be ready to give students credit for producing almost any kind of fiction or nonfiction as long as their writing has something to say and says it well. But even then, you do have objectives for their work—and you know this because you can imagine both successful and unsuccessful products that students might turn in. To begin with, you want students to write enough to say something worthwhile, and you want them to say it well enough to communicate with you, their reader. Stating your objectives helps both you and your students understand what you want them to do. Consider these examples:

> *Students will write an application, analysis, synthesis, or evaluation—in any style or genre and of at least 300 words—of any or all of the readings in this course*

and

> *Students will write in any style or genre a description, analysis, and/or evaluation of their summer—as it was or as it might have been.*

An assignment sheet and rubric can provide more information about the basis for evaluation and grading.

These kinds of wide-open writing assignments may be used as both objectives and assessments or as learning activities. In the case of the first example (writing about course readings), if you have taught students how to respond to readings intellectually and aesthetically and how to use various genres to make a point, this assignment can show you what your instruction has enabled them to do, functioning both as an objective and as an assessment for the course. If your plan is just to see how students handle the freedom to write in the manner the first objective describes without having received instruction, it can function as a diagnostic assessment (see Chapter 7) and probably as a learning activity, as well.

The second of the example objectives is a formal wording of the informal "Write about your summer, realistically or not, but give me something good to read." It, too, can be an objective *and* an assessment, if students have been explicitly taught how to tackle this kind of assignment, but as you'd be likely to give an assignment like this very early in the school year, it is less a statement of what they will know and be able to do as a result of instruction than a diagnostic assessment containing elements of a learning activity. In that case, their writing will be a practice piece that can show both you and them where they are in their writing development before instruction begins.

A Final Note

From an instructional designer's standpoint, both *reading* and *writing* are analogous to *learning* or *understanding*. Like learning and understanding, reading and writing are done across a broad spectrum of possibilities and at a range of levels. Because reading and writing are performed for others to see or hear, there is a risk of assuming that we've clearly determined a learning outcome when we say that students will read this or write that. This is a false assumption. If you imagine what the most gifted and engaged students might do with the assignment to read or write and contrast that with what the least gifted and engaged students might do, you can see that it really is necessary to set expectations for learning outcomes in reading and writing just as you do for other activities.

5

Checking the Validity of Objectives

The most direct way to check an instructional objective is to ask whether it is student-centered, is thinking-centered, and describes a performance that demonstrates learning. If the performance is something that's not directly observable—an analysis, for example—the teacher must ensure it can be readily demonstrated in an observable form, such as in writing or in a graphic organizer. If an objective meets these criteria, the chances are good that it is a solid, useful learning objective. However, there are other tests that address these criteria and can help you determine whether the objective states what students will know and be able to do.

We have already talked about two of these tests. First, there's Mager's (1984) Hey Dad test, described in Chapter 3. An objective that passes this test describes work that the student can demonstrate; it is student-centered and performance-centered. And what, specifically, Dad will watch determines whether or not the objective is thinking-centered. For example, "Hey, Dad! Watch me ride my bike!" demonstrates learning in the psychomotor domain rather than in the cognitive domain. But if the student performs a task that requires intellectual work, Hey Dad is a very helpful test.

Then there is the Principal in the Hall test. Like Hey Dad, it requires students to demonstrate their knowledge, and posits the principal standing in the hall outside the classroom and asking the students who emerge, "What did you learn in there today, and what can you do now that you couldn't do before?" There is a degree of professional intensity associated with administrators (and parents) asking students what they know and can do that helps many teachers see immediately whether their instructional objectives are viable.

Both these tests help to distinguish learning outcomes from learning activities. Both tests remind instructional designers to be sure that their objectives describe demonstrable skills and knowledge that the students take with them outside of the classroom.

Another test that can distinguish learning activities from learning outcomes is the Whaddya Know test. Once we realize that all the cognitive-performance verbs require the learner to demonstrate knowledge and thinking, we can see that a person must know something relevant and be thinking about it in order to show that he or she has achieved valid instructional objectives. Consequently, Whaddya Know prompts us to evaluate an instructional objective by responding to the question, "Does a person need to have meaningful knowledge about the subject matter in order to do whatever it is that this objective describes?"

Let's take a look how some of previously provided examples of unsatisfactory objectives fare when subjected to the Whaddya Know test. Consider:

Students will visit the Gettysburg museum.

Does a person need to have meaningful knowledge about this subject matter (the Battle of Gettysburg) in order to do this (visit the Gettysburg Museum)? No. A person does not have to know anything in order to visit a museum.

Now try this one:

Students will include a title page on their reports.

Do students need to have meaningful knowledge about the subject matter (the report) in order to include a title page on their report? Well, although students do need to know what a title page is in order to include one, they do not necessarily need to know anything about how to write a report or about the subject the report addresses.

How about this one?

Students will get a lesson on using Internet sources.

Clearly the answer is no. "Getting a lesson" does not require meaningful knowledge of Internet sources.

How do the three objectives about the periodic table that we looked at in Chapter 3 fare?

Students will recognize the importance of the periodic table.

Students will use the periodic table to make predictions about properties of elements.

Students will explain the arrangement of elements into groups and periods in the periodic table.

Does a person need to know something meaningful about the periodic table to recognize its importance? Not necessarily. If a student hears the teacher describing what a great tool the periodic table is and how much information it carries, the student may accept its importance without learning much else about it. On the other hand, a person *does* need have meaningful knowledge of the periodic table and the elements in order to use the table to predict properties of elements and to explain the arrangement of the elements.

If the answer to the Whaddya Know question is no, then what you have may be a good learning activity, but it is not a valid objective, because objectives describe what students know as a result of learning the lesson the teacher has taught.

Sample Validity Checks

Let's examine the validity of some objectives by applying the tests we've discussed.

1. "Students will differentiate common punctuation marks."

This instructional objective is student-centered, thinking-centered, and performance-centered. However, the verb "differentiate" may mean only that students will recognize that various punctuation marks are different from one another; that's a low level of learning. Distinguishing a comma from a semicolon, for example, doesn't require a meaningful level of knowledge about punctuation—it requires the barest minimum knowledge. If you want more, the objective should make that clear:

> *Students will correctly identify commas, periods, question marks, and exclamation marks as they encounter them in text.*

If you want students to know how to use punctuation, you could write better objectives by stating that directly:

> *Students will explain the uses of commas, periods, question marks, and exclamation marks*

> or

> *Students will use commas, periods, question marks, and exclamation marks correctly in paragraphs they compose.*

Because the more complex levels of learning and performance include those that are less complex, students who can use punctuation marks correctly will also be able to differentiate them.

Note that the verb "differentiate"—and many others like it, such as "identify," "describe," and "summarize"—may accurately describe a simple level of learning or a sophisticated one. For an example of a context in which differentiating would require a high degree of skill and knowledge, consider

Students will differentiate degrees of postmodern influence in contemporary writers.

This is another reminder that instructional designers make critically important decisions as they select and describe their learning goals for their students.

2. "Students will study the different motivations for founding colonial settlements in New England and Virginia."

Is it student-centered? Yes. It's arguably thinking-centered, but not in our sense of "thinking" as informed by Bloom's taxonomy, because studying may or may not entail much apprehending of new information. But this objective fails all three of our performance-centered tests. It fails the Principal-in-the-Hall test ("Well, we studied colonies, but I don't remember anything about them"). It fails the Hey Dad test ("Hey Dad, watch me study motivations for founding colonies!"). It fails the Whaddya Know test, as a person doesn't need to have any knowledge of colonial history in order to "study the motivations of the founders of the Virginia and New England colonies." There is no learning outcome in this objective—only a learning process that may or may not be successful.

To create instructional objectives from this statement, ask yourself what you want students to be able to do after they study. You might decide to amend the objective like this:

Students will compare and contrast colonists' motivations for founding settlements in New England and Virginia.

"Hey Dad, today we learned why colonists in New England and Virginia founded settlements where they did—and how those reasons were the same and different. Look at this chart I made showing why some colonists went to New England and some went to Virginia!" A student certainly needs to know something significant about colonial history in order to achieve this revised objective.

3. "Students will identify the major themes in the novel *The Lord of the Flies.*"

This objective clearly lays out the intellectual work the students must be able to do, focusing on students, their thinking, and their performance. It, like other acceptable cognitive objectives, passes the Hey Dad and Whad-dya Know tests.

The intellectual work here will require a sophisticated kind of demonstration, and the instructional designer will need to create an assessment to show students the form they'll use when identifying the novel's theme. After all, a theme is not something a student can point to on a page; identifying themes requires analysis and synthesis as well as interpretation. A student telling the principal, "I learned to identify themes in this novel, and I can show you how I do it" will probably describe a number of scenes, plot events, and characters, and when interpreted and synthesized, these scenes, plot events, and characters reveal themes. The instructional designer imagining what successful learners will be able to do will visualize students engaged in a wide-ranging, multilayered performance.

Here's an example of an essay prompt that would require students to show their ability to identify major themes in *The Lord of the Flies:* "William Golding wrote that he considered the theme of *The Lord of the Flies* to be 'an attempt to trace the defects of society back to the defects of human nature.' Decide whether you agree or disagree that this is a major theme of the novel. Then identify and support with textual evidence two or more different themes, and explain what relationship (supportive or oppositional) each bears to Golding's stated theme."

4. "Students will appreciate the differences and similarities among the major impressionist artists."

This one is student-centered, but it's not thinking-centered because the verb "appreciate" is too vague. When students achieve this objective—when they can "appreciate" the differences between the artists, what is it they will they be able to do?

If "appreciate" is used in the sense of "value," this objective is in the affective domain rather than the cognitive domain. If "appreciate" is used in the sense of "to be fully aware of," then, yes, it could serve as a general cognitive goal. However, it presents the same problem that using "understand" does: we can't see this "understanding"—this full awareness in the students' minds—and understanding is too general to be clearly demonstrated.

To pin the idea of "appreciate" down, we need to ask how students could demonstrate their awareness of differences and similarities in these artists' works. Then we might say

> *Students will list* [or identify, or describe, or explain] *the differences and similarities among the major impressionist artists*

or

> *Students will compare and contrast technique and subject matter in the works of major impressionist artists.*

The second of these revisions shows how the teacher has sharpened the focus to provide a clearer picture of what kind of learning and thinking a successful student will be able to demonstrate. The assessment that the teacher designs will show the exact form in which students will do their comparing and contrasting.

5. "Students will recognize the common prefixes that refer to number, such as *mono-, di-,* and *tri-.*"

Students who achieve this objective will be able to tell the principal, "I know that 'di' in 'dinitrogen' tells how many nitrogen ions there are." If recognizing these prefixes is adequate knowledge, this objective is acceptable. However, the students' ability to recognize something does not necessarily mean that they understand it or will be able to use it appropriately. If you want students to remember the meanings of these prefixes and use them when they are writing and speaking, then say so:

> *Students will use the common prefixes that refer to number*
> *(such as* mono-, di-, *and* tri-*) in writing and speaking.*

Note the use of the verb "use," which is associated with the Application level of Bloom's taxonomy and implies the ability to also employ the thinking skills at the levels beneath it—both Knowledge and Comprehension. The assessment that follows from this objective will detail the kinds of writing and speaking students will do to demonstrate their mastery of these prefixes.

6. "Students will experience the power of symbolism in the novel *The Scarlet Letter.*"

The idea behind this objective is affective rather than cognitive. Try Hey Dad, Principal in the Hall, and Whaddya Know. There are no clear passes on any of them. "Experience the power of" is a way of saying that students will be emotionally as well as intellectually impressed by the author's use of symbolism. To move to a clearer cognitive objective, we need (as always) to focus on students' learning and what they will come to know about symbolism in *The Scarlet Letter* rather than what they may come to feel about it. It can help to imagine a successful learner—an impatient realist, perhaps—who doesn't like symbolism but still needs to be able to

> *Explain how symbols are used in* The Scarlet Letter.

A student who can do this can also describe what symbols the author has incorporated into the telling of this story; symbols must be identified before they can be explained.

You might want students to

Explain how symbols affect [or contribute to] *the reader's experience of the novel*

or

Evaluate the role of the symbolism

but if you ask for these explanations and evaluations as the performance, you must be prepared for opinions that you don't agree with. Whatever you decide, pinning down clear instructional objectives reveals what you are going to teach, and if your objective is that students "experience the power of symbolism," you will be trying to teach them to feel something as well as to engage intellectually with it. It is understood that most English teachers encourage affective responses to literature, but they must be clear about what they are doing and about the inherent practical and moral difficulties associated with assessing and grading students' feelings. Cognitive objectives do not describe everything that is taught or learned, but they should be the sole basis for issuing achievement-based grades.

7. "Students will memorize the original 13 states and the largest cities in each."

This objective is student-centered and specific, but try the Principal in the Hall test on it. "We memorized the first 13 states" sounds like a promising beginning, but when the student says, "I'll show you what I can do," it requires moving on to a new verb (such as "write" or "tell") and leaving "memorize" behind. What does the need to bring in a new verb indicate? That "memorize" is not a performance-centered verb in this context, and that this objective actually refers to a learning activity rather than a learning outcome.

This issue merits a closer look. Memorizing is a process of taking in new information; it's an internal mental activity that prepares students for certain performances. Some kind of performance is needed to show that memorization has been done, so it is better to use descriptions of that performance instead of the term "memorize" in objectives. For example, after students have memorized this information, you may want them to *list* or *recite* the states and their cities. In that case, your objective may include the phrase "from memory" after *list* or *recite*. If you want students to apply the information they have memorized, you can ask them to *name and place* states and cities on an unlabelled map.

What we see in our original, then, is an objective stating something that is not quite at the endpoint of student learning. The distinction between memorizing and reciting seems small, but it is good professional practice to keep thinking about how students learn and how they will demonstrate their learning, and to be accurate in stating the results of your thinking. When you design learning activities for this lesson, you will align them with what you want students to do with memorized information.

8. "Students will be asked to work cooperatively with other students."

This is a description of *how* rather than *what* students will learn. It is not a description of what students will know and be able to do at the end of the lesson. The passive voice should immediately tip you to the objective's teacher-centered perspective.

Still, working cooperatively is an example of a skill that we want all our students to have, so if your students do not know how to do it, teaching them would be a valid use of class time. In that case, the yearlong objective could be something like this:

> *Students will work cooperatively in groups of three to identify the main ideas in texts, articulate opinions, and solve problems.*

You would need to give students sufficient practice in cooperative learning, and, as with all instructional objectives, you'd need to make sure students understand that they'll receive feedback on their performance and be evaluated on how well they do it.

Keep in mind, however, that even if you do not teach cooperative learning—and so do not assess it and do not include it in your instructional objectives—it's a valuable skill, and therefore falls into the category of important learning activities that students should keep practicing (like reading and writing and public speaking) in many different subjects. Not everything that students do and learn, nor everything you teach, must be included in instructional objectives.

9. "Students will realize that classification is the arrangement of objects, ideas, or information into groups, the members of which have one or more characteristics in common."

The first thing you may notice about this objective is that it contains detailed content information. Including this level of detail in an objective is not wrong, but doing so may shift your focus away from student thinking toward lists of information. Details of content can go elsewhere in the lesson plan—usually into assessments and plans for learning activities (see Chapters 7, 8, and 9).

Content aside, does this objective pass our three tests of validity? Clearly it doesn't pass the Hey Dad test; the verb "realize" is not specific enough to be used as an instructional objective, because it means "understand." What do you visualize students doing when they show you that they realize what classification means? You probably want students to say more to the principal in the hallway than "I now realize that classification is the arrangement of objects, ideas, or information into groups, the members of which have one or more characteristics in common." And how would they phrase the next part of their report of their learning—the "I'll show you my new skill" part?

There are a number of ways to revise this focus so that it's performance-centered. Perhaps you want students to be able to *describe* several examples of classification from their own experience and *define* the term. You might also want them to *identify* correct and incorrect examples of classification.

You might want them, when provided with an assortment of items, to be able to *classify* those items and *explain their reasoning*. Here's an objective that includes all of these desired outcomes and involves the highest levels of thinking on both Bloom's taxonomy (1956) and the updated version (Anderson et al., 2001): Synthesis and Create/Synthesize, respectively:

> *Students will create and use categories for the classification of disparate items and explain their reasoning.*

"Hey Dad, look at these categories I made for organizing this weird collection of stuff! Do you want me to tell you why they all make sense?"

10. "Students will know that a solute broken into small parts will dissolve in a solvent faster than the same amount of solute in a single solid mass."

The problem with this objective is that the cognitive verb—*know*—is too general. What do you want students to be able to do? What level of *knowing* are you aiming for? Do you want students just to recognize the truth of the objective's statement (as they would on a true-false test)? Do you want them to memorize what happens when a solute is broken into smaller parts and be able to answer the question "What happens when a solute is broken into smaller parts?" Do you want them to correctly predict what will happen when solutes and solvents are mixed in different ways? Is it important that they be able to explain why these phenomena occur? The verb "know," like the verb "understand," begs you to probe more carefully into what you want your students to achieve. A better, clearer choice might be this:

> *Students will explain why solutes of varying masses and surface areas dissolve at different rates.*

11. "Students will watch a video about music in Spain."

Try the Whaddya Know test on this objective. Does a person need to know or understand something significant about music or Spanish culture in order to watch a video? No, someone can watch a video without *any* prior knowledge of these topics, meaning this objective is not appropriately thinking-centered. The teacher's real objective is that students learn certain facts about Spanish music, not just that they keep their eyes open while the video plays (although staying awake is certainly a necessary prerequisite to learning the facts!). When the teacher focuses on the intellectual work that he wants students to do, it becomes obvious that the true instructional objective is something like this:

> *Students will describe traditional and contemporary music in Spain.*

The video is only a means to achieving that objective. If the video player breaks down, the lesson could still go on. Note, too, that the objective about the video fails the Hey Dad test: "Watch me watch this video!" is not what we want our students to be saying to their parents.

12. "Students will demonstrate ability to tell time (analog and digital) to the minute."

Student-centered? Yes. Performance-centered? Yes. Thinking-centered? Yes again. However, the phrase "demonstrate ability to" is unneeded verbiage. A simple "Students will tell time . . ." does the job. A similar situation is the following:

> *Students will demonstrate the correct procedure for retrieving documents from the Internet.*

This can also be phrased like this:

> *Students will retrieve documents from the Internet using the correct procedure.*

The wordier first version of this objective emphasizes the importance of students' using a procedure, but both versions express what students will know and be able to do at the end of the lesson.

The focus on wordiness here has purpose beyond style preferences. "Demonstrate" is another verb that must be considered carefully in context. If it is used by an instructional designer who hasn't quite decided exactly what students should know and do, the resulting objective will be unacceptably vague. Sooner or later the teacher must decide exactly how students will demonstrate their knowledge and what kind of knowledge it should be. Making those decisions allows the teacher to create a truly useful objective and then move to other decisions about assessment and instruction.

There are instances, however, in which "demonstrate" can accurately describe students' performance:

> *Students will demonstrate multiplication as repeated addition,*
> *and division as repeated subtraction.*

If you visualize a successful learner demonstrating these facts, you will see that the verb "explain" might also describe what you want the student to be able to do, but "demonstrate" connotes both reasoning and showing.

Characteristics of Good Instructional Objectives

The following summarizes the information about objectives that the chapters have laid out to this point. Use the questions listed to help you evaluate your own objectives and the objectives you encounter from other sources.

They are clear and specific.

Good objectives clearly and specifically state in student-centered language what students will know and be able to do at the end of the lesson. The instructional designer must ask

- What learning outcome am I stating in this objective?
- Can I visualize what a successful learner will be able to do?
- Have I distinguished between learning activities and learning outcomes?

• If the students achieve this objective, how will they complete this sentence: "Now, I am able to _____"?

They focus on thinking.

Good objectives describe intellectual work that students do. The instructional designer must ask

• Does this objective require the students to have knowledge about the subject matter and use that knowledge in some way? (Or ask the question in reverse: can a person who doesn't know anything significant about the subject achieve this objective?)

• As a teacher, can I explain to students, parents, and administrators what kinds of thinking this objective requires my students to do?

• What level of cognitive work (on Bloom's taxonomy) does this objective require?

• Does this objective describe ways of thinking about new knowledge rather than simply using previously learned knowledge?

Their mastery can be demonstrated.

Good objectives are assessable—meaning that the teacher can design a fair and valid way for students to demonstrate their mastery of every objective. The instructional designer must ask

• Does this objective describe—at least in general terms—what I want students to be able to do?

• Once students have achieved this objective, can I devise ways for the students to demonstrate this knowledge to an outside evaluator, such as the principal or the parents?

They are measurable.

Good objectives are measurable—meaning that the teacher can design a fair and valid way for students to demonstrate how well, or to what degree, they have achieved the objectives. The instructional designer must ask

- What do I visualize a successful learner being able to do as a result of this lesson?
- Does this objective, as stated, allow me to establish the depth or breadth of knowledge that is required for mastery?
- Can I visualize a reasonable level of performance on the aligned assessment task that is consistent with this objective?

They are (usually) aligned with standards.

Most of the time, good objectives are aligned with academic standards set forth by the state, the school district, and the school. The instructional designer must ask

- If a student achieves this objective, will that student have made progress toward mastery of a relevant academic standard?
- If this objective is not connected with state academic standards, can I explain to students, parents, and administrators why it is worth using school time to achieve?
- Taken together, do the objectives for a lesson or unit address all the important learning that students should do?

Now that we have carefully examined the purposes and characteristics of objectives, we are ready to take a close look at the process of creating them. The next chapter explains how to pull together your knowledge of objectives together with your content knowledge and construct clear learning outcomes for your students.

6

Creating Instructional Objectives

Creating objectives, as we noted in Chapter 1, is a critical part of the "deep design" work that teachers do. It's a process that requires teachers to first garner certain kinds of knowledge and then make clear decisions about how to use this knowledge.

Broadly speaking, an instructional designer needs four types of prerequisite knowledge to establish objectives:

- Knowledge of curriculum.
- Knowledge of lesson content.
- Knowledge of students.
- Knowledge of the vital role that objectives play in teaching and learning.

This list may leave you thinking, "If I knew all that, I'd know everything there is to know about teaching!" It's true that this prerequisite knowledge is extensive, and the fact that all this knowledge is necessary is a reminder that a successful instructional designer is in command of a great deal of information. However, simply knowing one's curriculum, lesson content, and students and grasping the importance of objectives will not automatically make a teacher a successful instructional designer. The key to making this happen is turning knowledge into successful lessons. That work begins with deciding the following:

- What you want students to learn in specific units and lessons.
- What extent and form of that learning they will be expected to achieve.
- How to state the results of your decisions in clear, concise language.

Creating objectives can be challenging, but it is a process that can be learned step by step and one that does become easier with practice. Furthermore, the process of creating objectives adds to teachers' professional knowledge, both in terms of the research they do into content and in terms of their subsequent determination of how their students will connect with that content. Creating meaningful objectives virtually always makes one a better teacher. The process even becomes enjoyable—a rewarding way for teachers to use their creativity and professional expertise.

A Closer Look at the Prerequisite Knowledge

The first prerequisite for creating strong instructional objectives is that you know your curriculum. It's the curriculum that will guide both the teacher's own content-knowledge development and decisions about what students will learn.

Begin your design work for each course, unit, or lesson by asking yourself which parts of the content area you will be teaching. Your school district's curriculum and the academic standards on which it is based will provide significant (if not always fully detailed) information about the areas of the discipline that students are required to learn. Additional guidance can be found in the standards created by professional organizations for the various disciplines, such as history, science, English, and mathematics. These organizations have created national objectives for their subjects, and these objectives are available online (see Appendix B).

The second prerequisite for establishing objectives is that you know the content of your lesson or unit well. Teachers need to be lifelong learners because, as Danielson (2007) notes, "a person cannot teach what he or she does not know" (p. 62). She adds that content "encompasses all aspects of a subject: concepts, principles, relationships, methods of inquiry, and outstanding issues" (p. 44).

The basis of your instructional plan is your own understanding of the content, and you may well need to investigate the subject of particular units or lessons further, both to fill in your content knowledge to your own satisfaction and to prepare more fully for helping your students develop an integrated, meaningful understanding.

The third prerequisite for creating objectives is that you know your audience—the students who will be learning what you teach. If you are designing instruction for students you haven't yet met, you will have to work with what you do know and can predict about them, based on your experience with other students, on what your colleagues can tell you (especially if you are a new teacher or new to the district), and on what you can learn from other sources.

As you plan, you must of course keep in mind that all good teachers are flexible and can respond to their students' learning needs as those needs become evident. Embedded in the professional knowledge of students is knowledge of how people learn and what they need in order to absorb new knowledge, make sense of it, and use it in a meaningful way.

The final prerequisite is to be clear in your own mind that objectives are a necessary foundation for making decisions about what you and your students should do in your time together. Clearly stated objectives are evidence that you have pinned down not only the *what* of student learning but also to some extent the *how* (e.g., students will work on problem solving or written explanations) and even some of the *why* (e.g., so they'll be able to perform tasks and use their abilities in certain ways). In addition, your objectives are the bedrock on which you will build assessments and learning activities for your students.

Step 1: Deciding What Students Should Learn

One of the challenges in thinking about what you want your students to learn is committing yourself (and your students) to specifics rather than remaining in the more forgiving realm of generalities, where it seems to be an open possibility that students might learn *everything*. Of course they cannot, so teachers must select what is most important. Curriculum guides and academic standards provide an overall view of course content, but it's teachers' responsibility to decide what to cover in specific units and daily lessons. Although it is useful to begin planning with a commonsense general statement of what you want students to know, learn, or understand, eventually you will need to make choices about what to include in your stated objectives, what to treat as supplementary, and what to omit altogether.

For an example of turning generalities into specifics, imagine yourself back on the Texas middle school planning team, designing the unit that includes a walking tour of the businesses in the students' community. Another standard this unit might address could be this one, for 7th grade social studies: Students will "describe how people from selected racial, ethnic, and religious groups attempt to maintain their cultural heritage while adapting to the larger Texas culture" (Texas Department of Education, 2010). As phrased, this standard presents a fairly general statement of what students will be able to do. To create a set of lessons that will help students achieve this goal, you and your fellow teachers must come up with objectives focused on learning about *specific* people "from selected racial, ethnic, and religious groups" and about the *specific* ways that these individuals "maintain their cultural heritage while adapting to the larger Texas culture." An informal expression of your more specific goal might be

Students should begin by learning about cultures we have right here by seeing and talking to people who value their heritage but also are fitting in with the Texas culture overall.

This is an example of beginning to translate a state's general goal into specific objectives that tie the unit to the standard. You might continue this work by identifying individual families in the community who would be willing to share their cultural practices with the students, along with examples of community events that reflect these practices. Then, ultimately, the objectives for the unit would include

> *Students will compare and contrast ways that Texans of Hispanic, German, and Native American heritage maintain their cultural traditions*

and

> *Students will compare and contrast the ways that Texans of Hispanic, German, and Native American heritage adapt to Texas culture.*

In the actual unit plan, you could use descriptions of assessments and learning activities to clarify that the sources of information about these ethnic groups will include some local citizens.

Various Ways of Making Content Decisions

The larger the unit of study, the more decisions you need to make about content. However, the process of planning for a large unit of instruction can be the same as that for a small one, or even for a single lesson. Begin by stating in your own terms what you want students to learn. If you begin with general overall statements, gradually tighten your focus on what is embedded in those statements. For each statement that you make, such as "Students have to know about the U. S. Civil War" (clearly an example of a large unit), ask what information underlies that achievement. In this example, you might answer that students will need to know why and when the war began, how it proceeded, and what the consequences were. They will need to know the major figures, the roles these people played, and so on. Step by step, you will build a composite picture of the knowledge that you want each student to have by the end of the unit.

People's minds work in a variety of ways, and although establishing objectives is the first order of business, not everyone begins working on objectives in the same way. There are various approaches that can get you where you need to go.

Option 1: Begin with the end in mind.

A helpful technique in pinning down desired learning outcomes is to imagine successful students demonstrating and using their new knowledge in the future. What would you want them to take from this unit to the next one or to the next course in the history curriculum? What would you like for them to show to an outside evaluator? What would your students need to know and be able to do at the end of the unit to make you feel satisfied with the content decisions that you made?

This approach is decision making by backtracking from the desired end. Wiggins and McTighe (2005) provide detailed steps, including worksheets, for designing this way. They refer to it as "backward design" because the process begins by identifying the final outcome. Any design process that begins with creating objectives follows this pattern, and it's so widely and successfully used as a method for planning instruction that it could now be called "standard design."

Option 2: Chose a focus, and move outward.

An alternative approach is to begin with a particular focus. Instead of thinking about everything you want students to know about the Civil War, you might begin with an image of Abraham Lincoln that jumps into your mind. Ask yourself what you want your students to know about this particular part of the content. Maybe you want them to know about Lincoln's character, the conflicts he faced, the decisions he made, the values he held, and the consequences of his presidency. Now, with these generalities in mind, you can move on to the specifics: what would your students need to know in order to acquire this picture of Lincoln, the man and the president? With Lincoln at the center of your initial conceptual map, you can work outward to include more and more of the information that is important for students to know about the Civil War.

Option 3: Select powerful details, and make connections.

Some people prefer to begin with memorable details that are interesting and important to them, such as Harriet Tubman's vivid dreams and visions that may have resulted from her childhood head injury. If this describes you, ask yourself why each detail is important and what larger picture it is part of. Gradually move outward to connect these facts, artifacts, people, or events to one another and to larger themes until you have formed a conceptual map of the required content.

Another example of this approach is a science teacher who knows that her students love the demonstration in which she explodes a balloon filled with hydrogen. The chemical combination of hydrogen and oxygen is just one example of a chemical reaction, but by working outward from the principles that this explosion demonstrates, she can prepare her students to see it as more than just an exciting flash of light and loud noise. She can use the explosion as an opportunity for students to explore combustion, molecular structure, exothermic reactions, and how to balance chemical equations. However, although her thinking about course objectives begins with this demonstration of combustion, her final design of the unit will not necessarily place it at the beginning. Instead, she will incorporate it where it will provide the greatest contribution to students' learning.

Option 4: Begin with an activity, and explore its purpose.

It is also possible to begin with a particular activity that you want students to do. For example, you may have a field trip or a performance for other teachers' classes in mind. You may, for example, want your students to transform the classroom into a rain forest or "pi World." If you begin here, ask yourself what students will know at the end of the experience. Your answer to this question reveals the purposes for the experience, which is another way of stating your instructional objectives for it. You also should ask yourself what knowledge and skills students will need in order to do this activity well and, thus, achieve these instructional objectives. Your answers to these follow-up questions will help you identify further knowledge that you want students to learn.

If the activity is a culmination of a unit, it can serve the same role in your planning that a broad statement such as "I want students to understand the course and significance of the Civil War" serves. It is an end point toward which you and your students are headed. If the activity will occur somewhere in the middle of the unit, it can serve the same planning purpose that Lincoln served in the second example: an anchor in the body of the unit or a theme that runs through it.

It doesn't really matter where you begin in your decision making about content. Just keep exploring your subject, noting what you think students can and should learn until you are satisfied that you have noted it all. Before, during, and after your design work, revisit the academic standards and the district curriculum guides to make sure the relevant content is addressed in your instructional plan.

The process of deciding what students should learn takes time and patience. Brainstorming with a colleague can help. Draw on as many resources as you can, such as books, videos, colleagues, the Internet, community members, and of course, academic standards. Do not cut corners, for this work is essential. It creates the foundation of your instruction; it lays out the parameters of the map you will use to navigate your (and your students') way through this material. Only when the content is selected will you be ready to design the rest of the instruction.

Step 2: Choose the Depth and Breadth of Learning

Establishing the content of your unit or lesson plan is the first step. The next step is to determine exactly what kind of learning you want your students to do.

As with deciding what the content of your unit should be, deciding what extent and form of learning you want students to be responsible for can be an exercise to share with colleagues, whether in person, online, or through books or other media. Wiggins and McTighe (2005), for example, provide an excellent discussion of how to establish priorities for curriculum content, asking readers to classify all that they want to teach into three categories: what is "worth being familiar with" (and thus requires only minimal investigation), what is "important to know and do," and what is "necessary for enduring understanding" (p. 10). You don't have to make these decisions in isolation; you will use the academic standards, your school's curriculum, and advice from colleagues to guide you. But you do need to determine what you will be teaching so that you know what you want to see from your students as they gain new skills and knowledge and so that they will know what you expect of them.

Use Bloom's taxonomy to help you decide what level of thinking and learning is appropriate for your students and the content they will learn. As an example, consider the differences in student learning outcomes among these three objectives:

> *Students will identify kinds of precipitation.*
>
> *Students will explain how water enters a watershed.*
>
> *Students will describe the major watersheds in the United States.*

Each requires a broader span of knowledge than the one that precedes it. All, however, require students to have a command of a set of facts but not to engage in higher levels of thinking.

To move learning to these higher levels, we would need to ask students to do more with the information they have:

> *Students will analyze the effects of types and quantities of precipitation in various geographic areas.*
>
> *Students will explain the relationship between a watershed and the life-forms within it.*
>
> *Students will evaluate the impact of human activity on specific watersheds.*

Establishing appropriate objectives for your lessons does require careful consideration of your various choices, in both content selection and in levels of thinking. This work will reward you by giving you clarity and confidence about what you will be teaching and how you will be teaching it. You will know what you are looking for in students' learning, and you will be able to guide individuals to the desired outcome.

Step 3: Express Objectives in Clear, Precise Language

Now it is time put your decisions about what your students should learn into the language of objectives. For a review of the requirements for putting objectives into words, see Chapters 3 and 4. The chief point to remember is that the language must focus on both students' thinking and the performance that thinking will allow.

Beginning with Simple Objectives

To start, choose a relatively simple learning outcome that you want your students to achieve. For this exercise, a "simple" learning outcome is one that you can easily visualize a successful student demonstrating. For example, students might recite poems or addition facts. They might use knowledge of phonics to sound out new words. They might perform a procedure in a lab exercise. Take a minute to visualize one of your successful learners after a lesson you will teach. What do you see them doing?

Write down what you are imagining—maybe "students reciting the alphabet" or "students using math manipulatives to divide fractions." At this point, you are just describing the successful learner's behavior, and you don't need to worry about how you are wording your description.

Once you have written down a statement of what your successful students can do, examine it to see if it would be a valid objective: a finished statement of the learning outcome you want. Here are the questions to ask:

• *Does the statement have a student-centered point of view?* Does it describe of what your students can do—or are doing—at the end of the lesson? If you're visualizing students using their knowledge, your answer to this question will almost certainly be yes.

• *Does the statement describe a learning outcome rather than a classroom exercise or activity?* As recommended in Chapter 2, put the phrase "at the end of the lesson" at the beginning of your statement and see if it still makes sense. Even if students would need weeks of practice to be able to do what your statement describes, that's OK. It still makes sense to say, "At the end of the lesson, students will recite the alphabet." It just happens to be a long lesson that students work on intermittently and practice throughout the school year.

• *Does the statement describe appropriate thinking?* Does your description include a verb associated with some kind of intellectual activity? If you are unsure, check a list of verbs built from Bloom's taxonomy and see if the one you've used in your description reflects the level of learning you are visualizing. Try out several other verbs to find one that most accurately describes the learning you want. Even if the verb doesn't seem to require much intellectual work (say, "recite" in the description "Students are reciting the alphabet"), you can check by asking yourself whether a student who didn't know anything about the topic area (the alphabet) could do the task. The answer here must be no. Students must know something in order to recite. If your statement needs refining to meet these criteria, tinker with it until it passes the tests described in Chapter 5.

Tackling More Complex Objectives

Once you're comfortable expressing very simple learning outcomes in clear, precise language, try using this visualization process with a more complex objective that requires more knowledge and more sophisticated thinking. Look to the higher levels of Bloom's taxonomy—Analysis, Synthesis, Evaluation, and Creation, which require broader and deeper thinking and draw on more knowledge. For example, you may want students to analyze the causes of a historical event or of a natural phenomenon, like lightning or the effects of heat. Analysis requires taking something apart to examine its components, and students tasked with analyzing the causes of conflict in a story must look beneath the surface of the characters' behavior and identify the forces at work. What might that kind of thinking look like, in terms of physical performance? Visualize a successful learner doing this. Imagine what the student would be able to say, write, draw, or act out to reveal the results of their analytical efforts. You might end up with something like this:

> *Students will explain how character, culture, and historical circumstances led to the deaths of Romeo and Juliet* [or of Adolf Hitler and Eva Braun].

As you develop your objective for more advanced learning, try out different kinds of knowledge and skills that you can imagine your students demonstrating. What do you want them to say to the principal in the hallway about what they've learned? Whatever it is, if it's what you want, and if it's aligned with academic standards, use it as the basis of your learning objective. Don't be satisfied with thinking that you just want students to be able to explain the basics of a concept; imagine *exactly* what you want to hear them say or see them do. Specify in your mental image the words your students will use, and pin down the learning outcome those words reveal.

Analyzing Academic Standards and Translating Them into Objectives

Once you are able to state objectives for the learning that you know your students must do, the next level of challenge is to generate objectives from academic standards.

Choose a standard (or part of one) and decide whether it is specific enough to be an objective as written. Many academic standards are too broad to be used as objectives. History standards, for example, commonly refer to broad concepts such as "change and continuity" or "cultural conflicts." It's necessary to study specific examples in order to understand these concepts, so when you are creating objectives from standards like these, focus on specific changes or specific examples of continuity, and visualize a student who understands why and how these are important. What can that student describe or explain?

PRACTICE EXERCISE: Translating Standards to Student Learning

This is a complicated step, so let's pause for practice, working with some of the U.S. Common Core Standards, created by the Common Core State Standards Initiative (CCSSI). The first example, for grade 2 language arts, has been analyzed and translated into objectives for you.

1. "Read grade-level text with purpose and understanding" (CCSSI, 2010a, p. 16).

Translating this standard into an objective is challenging, because the ability to read "with purpose and understanding" describes the successful student's mental state—something that's very difficult to observe. But let's try visualizing a 2nd grader who is doing those things. What might that student do or say? How might a child demonstrate or express a sense of purpose and understanding?

There are really two outcomes here: (1) demonstrating a sense of purpose and (2) demonstrating understanding. To get at purpose, we could ask a child directly, "Why are you reading this?" Then the objective becomes something like this:

> *Students will explain their purposes for reading the*
> *assigned text.*

We can imagine all kinds of answers children might give in response to our question: "Because I have to" and "To stay out of trouble and do what the teacher wants" and "Because I get to sit on a pillow in the reading corner and get away from Bobby" and "To get good at reading so my mom will stop worrying about it" or the simple "It's reading time." The art of teaching, and the art of thinking about student learning, suggest that all of these purposes may be relevant to individual children. The academic standard, however, is presumably intended to evoke a purpose in the cognitive domain. So that's where we'll put our attention when writing the objective. This means tightening the focus:

> *Students will explain what information or experiences they*
> *expect to get from reading the assigned text.*

When we locate this objective embedded within the standard, our own responsibility to our students becomes clearer. We need to prepare the students with some prereading orientation so they can say, "This is going to tell me how caterpillars turn into butterflies" or "This is a story about rockets, and I want to shoot off a rocket like my brother does." When students have enough experience with text to use titles, illustrations, and other clues to predict what the reading will give them, they can do their own preparation and set their own purposes for reading. Until that time, they need help in finding purposes in the cognitive domain that coexist with their other purposes in other domains.

The next part of the standard focuses on getting students to read with understanding. "Reading with understanding" is a vague phrase that doesn't tell us what level or type of understanding the successful student will demonstrate, but we can begin establishing the objective by saying that

Students will describe the information or narrative of the text.

And it's easy to make this generic description specific to a particular text:

Students will describe how caterpillars turn into butterflies
or
Students will retell the story of a girl who launched her first rocket.

Deriving useful objectives from standards frequently requires translating the intellectual work implied in the standard into observable student behavior. To make this translation, remember to focus on the student's thinking. Imagine that he or she is thinking in the way that the standard requires. Then ask yourself what you, the teacher, could do to prompt that student to speak or act in a way that clearly demonstrates the desired thinking. In the case of reading "with purpose and understanding," the desired thinking and the behavior that demonstrates it will, of course, become more complex as students become more experienced readers.

Now it's your turn. Here are some other common core standards for you to practice with. For a link to common core standards by discipline, please see Appendix B. Note that some of the verbs used in standards, such as "understand" and "recognize," are not specific enough to describe clear student learning outcomes. When you visualize students achieving the understanding or recognition, describe more precisely what thinking they are doing and what that thinking allows them to do.

Even if language arts and math are not among the subjects that you teach or if the specific objectives here are not good matches for your grade level, try working with these standards as an exercise in getting at the intention of the standard and then experiment with stating that intention as a functional objective. The more you practice bridging the distance between standards and students' learning, the more obvious and automatic the process becomes.

Language Arts Standards

2. "Explain how an author develops the point of view of the narrator or speaker in a text" (CCSSI, 2010a, p. 36).

3. "Determine an author's point of view or purpose in a text and analyze how the author distinguishes his or her position from that of others" (CCSSI, 2010a, p. 39).

4. "Analyze the author's purpose in providing an explanation, describing a procedure, or discussing an experiment in a text" (CCSSI, 2010a, p. 62).

Math Standards

5. "Develop understanding of fractions as numbers. Understand a fraction $\frac{1}{b}$ as the quantity formed by 1 part when a whole is partitioned into b equal parts; understand a fraction $\frac{a}{b}$ as the quantity formed by a parts of size $\frac{1}{b}$. (Expectations in this domain are limited to fractions with denominators 2, 3, 4, 6, and 8.)" (CCSSI, 2010b).

6. "Develop understanding of statistical variability. Recognize a statistical question as one that anticipates variability in the data related to the question and accounts for it in the answers. *For example, "How old am I?" is not a statistical question, but "How old are the students in my school?" is a statistical question because one anticipates variability in students' ages.* Understand that a set of data collected to answer a statistical question has a distribution which can be described by its center, spread, and overall shape. Recognize that a measure of center for a numerical data set summarizes all of its values with a single number, while a measure of variation describes how its values vary with a single number" (CCSSI, 2010c).

7. "Perform arithmetic operations with complex numbers. Know there is a complex number i such that $i^2 = -1$, and every complex number has the form $a + bi$ with a and b real" (CCSSI, 2010d).

In future chapters, you will have opportunities to use the objectives that you created here. Keep track those that you are interested in using as the basis for a full lesson plan.

7

Developing Assessments

Assessments, like all other elements of teaching, proceed logically and directly from thinking-focused objectives aimed at securing intellectual gains. Learning to design strong assessments is significantly easier and faster than learning to establish strong objectives because the difficult foundational work has already been done.

Before we look at how to develop assessments, we need to consider what, exactly, assessment is and the various forms it can take.

What Is Assessment?

Assessment is the process and product of determining whether students have learned what they were expected to learn from instruction. From the teacher's point of view, anything that reveals what students are learning, or how well they have learned, can be considered an assessment. When students ask or answer questions, they are showing something about their knowledge of the subject. When students write a reflective journal entry, they are providing a look at the sense they are making of a topic. When students use new information to create essays, song lyrics, posters, digital slides, answers to test questions, or advertising campaigns, they are demonstrating their understanding and level of mastery of the content. All of these processes and products are assessments if the teacher uses them to gather data about the students' learning. From the students' point of view, any method of showing the teacher what they do and don't know is an assessment.

All teachers know that simply delivering information, coming up with activities, or otherwise providing opportunities for students to master learning objectives does not always result in the intended learning (hence the wry comment heard in faculty lunchrooms: "I taught them, but they didn't learn"). Assessment data can show us what skills and understanding have not transferred and indicate where we need to focus our attention in order to close gaps in the teaching-learning process.

Teachers have many choices about what kinds of assessments to use and need to make careful decisions about which assessment will best serve the ultimate goal of student success in learning. Assessment terminology can make a beginner's head swim, but that needn't happen if the logic behind the names is made clear. There are two basic ways of organizing assessments: by application and by format.

Assessment Application

Assessment application depends on *purpose*—the kind of information the assessment is intended to gather—and the *use* to which that information will be put. When you're talking about *diagnostic assessment, formative assessment, summative assessment, program assessment,* or *standards/benchmark assessment,* you're talking about assessment application.

Diagnostic assessment

Diagnostic assessment is any assessment that is used before the new learning begins. Its purpose is to inform the teacher what students know at a point before the next stage of their learning gets underway. Diagnostic assessment is most frequently used at the beginning of a semester or at the beginning of a unit or lesson, but it can be used during a unit or lesson if the teacher suspects that students don't have necessary background knowledge and are, therefore, not yet ready to take the next step toward mastery. Diagnostic assessments are generally not graded, as their purpose is preparation for teaching and learning new material.

A good general example of diagnostic assessment would be a 4th grade teacher kicking off a new school year by asking students to demonstrate their command of mathematical facts and concepts learned in 3rd grade. The results of this assessment will tell the teacher where each student stands in relation to the math curriculum and identify those students who need review and practice with earlier content. Even if the teacher begins 4th grade math lessons with a diagnostic assessment, she might decide in January (or at any time during the school year) to conduct another diagnostic assessment focused on the background knowledge needed for the particular unit coming up next.

Diagnostic assessments can take any form that will allow the students to show what they know and allow the teacher to gather the appropriate data about what students know. But it's important to remember that a teacher can use any task students engage in to "diagnose" skill and knowledge levels, regardless of whether the task was originally intended to serve that purpose. So while it's unlikely that a teacher would use a complex task, such as writing a research report, for a diagnostic assessment, if students' reports demonstrate weak research skills, a lack of a particular writing skill, and little knowledge of how to assemble a research report, the assignment might serve as diagnostic assessment by informing the teacher that the students need more instruction, practice, and feedback in these areas. The students' first attempts at writing research reports would then be regarded as their demonstration of what they need to learn as much as, or more than, a demonstration of what they had learned.

Formative assessment

Formative assessment is used during the learning process. Its purpose is to inform the teacher and the students how well the learning is going. Any format may be used—something as informal as oral questions in class during the lesson or as formal as a written quiz or essay.

Formative assessment can be tightly structured to focus on a particular concept or skill, as when the teacher says, "Everyone take four minutes to solve this next problem independently," or it can be wide open, as in "Take out your journals and tell me everything you know about the story we are reading." What makes formative assessment *formative* is that the teacher and the students use the data it generates to shape further instruction and learning. Some teachers do use formative assessment for grading, but with this assessment application, the real objective is to uncover and make sure the students are informed of their own progress—through teachers' comments or another way of showing them what they are understanding or doing well, and what they are struggling with or misunderstanding. Students need to know how well they are doing at least as much as the teacher does, and a key benefit of formative assessment is that students get this information at a point at which they can more easily get their learning back on course before the subject is set aside and a new unit begins. With guidance, students can come to play a very active role in formative assessment by taking the measure of their own learning and then taking steps to become more skilled and knowledgeable.

Most teachers are constantly assessing how their students' learning is progressing through such seemingly simple and natural means as watching facial expressions and body language; listening to students' comments, questions, and answers; reading journal entries; or checking homework. This kind of informal data gathering becomes formative assessment when the teacher uses that data to inform or guide instructional adjustments within the lesson or unit that's underway.

If you see a connection between formative assessment and diagnostic assessment, you're right; both gather information about where the student stands and prompt the teacher to decide which instructional steps will help students master the objectives. The key distinction is in the timing of the assessment rather than in its use or character. Diagnostic assessment occurs before teaching; formative assessment occurs during teaching.

Summative assessment

Summative assessment is designed and administered to "sum up" learning that has taken place during a lesson, a unit, or a course. The data it generates typically serve as the basis for a grade, a certificate, a degree, or any other marker of achieved learning. Basically, summative assessment is a form of final judgment on how well the student has learned and, by extension, how well the teacher has taught. One of the purposes of summative assessment is to help distinguish successful students, teachers, and schools from those that haven't been as successful, in the form of ratings such as grades or test scores.

In contrast to diagnostic and formative assessment, summative assessment does not play a direct role in the teaching or learning process, as the time when students can improve their achievement in that unit or course is past. But in the longer run, summative assessment can be used to help improve learning and teaching, as when a student is inspired to try harder next semester, when a teacher decides to use a new method of instruction, or when schools decide to make changes in hopes of improving student achievement. For example, consider state standardized tests, which are considered to be summative assessments. The scores are a permanent record of student achievement levels on the day the tests were administered. However, these tests also function as formative assessment when the school district analyzes the resulting data to make decisions about curriculum, staff development, and other policies.

Program assessment and standards assessment

Two other applications of assessment merit brief attention in this discussion: *standards* (or *benchmark*) *assessment,* the purpose of which is to find out how well students are achieving the state academic standards, and *program assessment,* which is used to find out whether students who complete a program have achieved the goals of the program and whether they are successful in the job the program was designed to prepare them for. The data that either of these assessments generates can be used in a diagnostic, formative, or summative manner and can focus on the individual student, the program, or the institution.

A final note on assessment applications: be aware that some educators use the word "assessment" to mean diagnostic or formative assessment and use the word "evaluation" to mean summative assessment.

Assessment Formats

We've talked about assessment application, which is dependent on purpose, and now it's time to consider assessment formats—various ways of grouping and describing the myriad forms these data-gathering instruments can take. In this section, we'll look at terms and descriptions that tend to be used most often, including *traditional assessments, alternative assessments, performance assessments,* and *authentic assessments.*

Traditional assessments

Traditional assessments have been used by schoolteachers for generations and include essays and various types of written tests, including multiple choice, fill-in-the-blank, short answer, and matching. These written assessments may be considered in two major subgroups—*selected-answer* or *constructed-answer,* depending on whether the test-taker selects an answer from a number of choices (e.g., multiple choice) or constructs and provides an answer, which might be anything from a few words or numbers to pages of equations or text. See McTighe and Ferrara (2000) for a concise, helpful discussion of these and other features of traditional test formats.

Traditional assessments may also take the form of an oral examination or an oral recitation of what the student has learned. An example of traditional oral examination and recitation is described in Laura Ingalls Wilder's *Little Town on the Prairie,* set in the 1880s. In contemporary American schools, oral examinations and recitations have become relatively rare, probably because they take a good deal of time and because class sizes are so large that listening to every student would be a tedious business for teacher and students alike.

Alternative testing formats

A number of alternative testing formats have emerged in response to criticism that traditional test formats are poor tools for determining how well a student truly understands material and can apply it to real-life situations. Alternative forms of assessment include group projects, portfolios of student work, performances, demonstrations, and other evidence of student learning. Any assessment that isn't traditional can be labeled "alternative." Two terms that are commonly used in connection with such alternative assessment are *performance assessment* and *authentic assessment.*

Performance assessments are designed to measure how well students can apply what they have learned; the emphasis is on what students can do with their knowledge rather than what they can simply recall or recognize as being the right answer in a written test. Although written tests can be designed to assess students' performance of skills, such as solving problems, analyzing, and evaluating (many questions on standardized tests do this), students' ability to perform some tasks can be measured more directly through performance assessment. For example, the reasoning goes, if students need to know how to write business letters and how to determine the level of pollution in a river, it makes sense to ask them to demonstrate that knowledge by actually writing letters and measuring pollution rather than by taking a written test on these topics. An even better performance assessment of these skills would be to ask them to write and send a letter to an existing business for a real purpose and to collect water samples from a body of water to determine the types and possible origins and consequences of pollution.

Authentic assessments require students to deal with realistic situations or problems—that is, situations or problems that occur outside classrooms and schools. The more closely a performance assessment matches a task that people do in "the real world," the more authentic it is said to be.

Conceptually, authentic assessments and performance assessments are very similar. The two terms just draw attention to different aspects of this kind of assessment. Of the two, performance assessments are more likely to occur in the classroom and may even take the form of traditional written tests—provided the questions require students to solve problems, apply and interpret data, or otherwise use skills in a realistic way. Authentic assessments are more likely to take place outside the classroom.

The term "authentic assessment" is an implied criticism of traditional school tests, since it implicitly puts school tests in an imagined category of "inauthentic assessment." An argument against "inauthentic assessment" is that almost nowhere in the adult world are people asked to take multiple-choice tests or write essays on literary criticism in a severely limited period of time without access to any collaboration or other resources. Furthermore, students taking school tests traditionally get only one chance to prove that they have learned the material. In the outside world, people generally do not face these restrictions; they usually have time to think about problems, consult with others, and revise the products they create. Because the purpose of schooling is to prepare young people to be successful adults, proponents of authentic assessments argue that we should be giving them practice in the skills and knowledge they will need in the future. Authentic assessments are also believed to be more engaging for students, as they permit students to demonstrate their skills and knowledge in a more natural and personal way—by doing—than is usually possible in a traditional assessment format that requires students to work within the language the teacher has chosen for questions on a test. See Wiggins and McTighe (2005) for an extended discussion and examples of the many ways that students can express their understanding.

Your choice of assessment format depends on what kind of learning you want to measure. For example, basic factual information can often be measured very efficiently by written tests. The amount of time available both for students to complete the assessment and for you to review the assessment data must factor into your decisions, as well. Traditional test formats usually require significantly less time than other kinds of assessments. As Wiggins and McTighe (2005) explain in *Understanding by Design,* a range of assessment formats produces the most complete picture of a student's learning, and this range includes traditional written tests.

Student success requires assessment formats that will allow them to demonstrate what they do and do not know clearly and reliably. A teacher must choose the format that will best suit the learning being displayed and the students displaying it. And remember that whatever format you choose can be used for the purpose of diagnostic, formative, or summative assessment.

Assessment Design

Assessment is a direct, logical step in the instructional process that is necessary to ensure that students achieve the outcomes your objectives describe.

A suitably direct, logical way to begin creating an assessment is to visualize a successful learner and ask, "What can this student do to show me that he has achieved the objective?" More specifically, you can ask, "What can this student say, write, or create? What questions can he answer? What tasks can he perform? Given the kind of thinking that the objective describes, how can the student prove that he is doing that thinking?" All these questions are tools for identifying the most appropriate way for students to demonstrate their thinking and learning.

Work from Your Objectives

A well-written objective is the best tool for helping you to imagine a successful student demonstrating the thinking and learning you hope to see. A poorly written objective, by contrast, usually leaves blanks or fuzziness where the details of thinking and performing should be. Consider the following objective, which we established back in Chapter 3 as one that needs revision:

Students will recognize the importance of the periodic table.

If the creator of this objective did not see right away that it was unfinished, trying to design an assessment would make its problems obvious. What can students do to demonstrate their recognition of the importance of the periodic table? What can they say or write? How can they demonstrate that they are doing the kind of thinking the objective requires? What format could their recognition-of-importance take?

Going by this objective, the imagined successful learner has only to say, "I know that the periodic table is important because it shows a lot of information about the elements." In fact, the student who can say, "I recognize the importance of the periodic table," has presumably achieved the objective. Attempting to design an assessment of this unpolished objective makes it obvious that it does not describe what intellectual work students will do. It does not guide the teacher and students toward the desired learning outcomes. If what the teacher really wants is for students to use information presented in the periodic table, both the objective and its assessment must say so.

The two improved versions of the objective make it much easier to visualize assessment tasks:

Students will use the periodic table to make predictions about properties of elements.

Students will explain the arrangement of elements into groups and periods in the periodic table.

We'll consider the first revision first and visualize students using the periodic table to make predictions about properties of elements. What will they be doing? Well, they will be making predictions about particular properties of particular elements, and they will be expressing those predictions in a particular format. This is an important point: your assessment statement should articulate not only the kind of thinking students will engage in (here, *predicting*, an Application-level skill) but also the specific task or tasks that will prompt or guide that thinking, like this:

In response to questions on a worksheet, students will use the periodic table to make predictions about the relative melting points of metals.

Turning to the second revision of the objective, imagine students explaining the arrangement of elements, and then identify a format that will allow them to do this:

Students will use writing and graphic display in a poster to explain the arrangement of elements into groups and periods in the periodic table.

Designing an assessment, like stating an objective, requires focus.

Watch for Incomplete Assessment Descriptions

In the examples we've just looked at, a teacher might be tempted to write simply "worksheet" or "poster" for the assessment, but that would be a mistake. Taking the time to both identify the assessment format and specify what students will do within that format to show their achievement of the objective is the best way to maintain a focus on student thinking.

Simply writing down "worksheet" or "poster" leaves open the possibility that any worksheet or poster will do. On the morning of this lesson, a teacher thinking, "Oh, that's right, I need a worksheet for today, so I'd better get one together," is probably less likely to carefully align the assessment task with the objective than is a teacher who creates the worksheet questions when the objective is newly written and fresh in mind. The worksheet developed when a teacher is thinking about instructional design is also more likely to be a valid assessment than is the one hastily put together in the pressure to prepare for class. When creating an assessment, give yourself time and space to think.

This may be the most common incomplete assessment description there is:

> *Students will take a test.*

The phrasing just postpones the necessary work of figuring out what test questions will assess students' knowledge appropriately. Contrast the above with a complete assessment description:

> *On a written test, students will describe local natural resources in answers to short-essay questions.*

The main reason test questions should be written in the planning stage, before the learning activities are chosen, is so that the teacher can match these questions to the thinking and knowledge students need to have to meet the objectives for the lesson or unit. When teaching about local natural resources, for example, the teacher will be able to keep the test questions he's written in mind and guide students' learning in the desired direction— toward standards mastery.

Beginning teachers are advised to create assessments after they have established the objective and before they move on to choosing learning activities. The wisdom of this design progression is simple: knowing the end points for learning is good way to ensure you provide students with what they need in terms of instruction so that they can reach that end point. But this is not the only way to approach or achieve effective instructional design. As long as a teacher understands the purposes for and elements of each part of the design—objectives, assessments, learning activities, and standards—the elements of a lesson plan can be created in any order. An expert designer, for example, will be able to determine the objective based on an assessment and will be able to determine the academic standard by seeing either the assessment or the objective. Seeing even one part of the lesson can give an expert a good idea of where the learning is headed and what students will be able to do at the end of it.

Find and Close Gaps Between the Objective and Its Assessment

Gaps between objectives and assessments occur when the instructional designer thinks in general rather than specific terms about assessment tasks. Just as fine-tuning objectives requires thinking specifically (even when the content knowledge is broad), so fine-tuning assessments requires ensuring that associated activities line up with specific objectives rather than just the larger body of content knowledge. Gaps can also occur when "inherited" or habitual learning activities and assessments don't mesh cleanly with standards—a situation that faces experienced teachers, as well as beginners.

Consider this state benchmark for 5th graders in Oregon: "Students will identify the primary functions of federal, state, and local governments" (Oregon Department of Education, 2001). Long-standing tradition within many Oregon elementary schools links this standard with a particular learning activity—a field trip to the state capitol. (Note, also, that a field trip like this can be an example of beginning your instructional design process with a specific activity in mind. See Chapter 6, p. 92.) When it comes to assessing what students learned from the field trip, however, the instructional designer can find it challenging to align assessment tasks closely with the benchmark. Take a look at the following assessment options. Which would provide evidence of students' progress toward achievement of the "state government" part of the standard?

- Upon returning to school, students will discuss with the teacher what they saw, did, and learned on the trip.
- Students will draw pictures to go into a hallway display of information about their trip.
- Students will write letters to their state representatives or senators mentioning what they learned from and liked about the visit.
- Students will read about the functions of state government and identify points in the reading that connect with something they saw or heard in the capitol building.

Unfortunately, none of these activities would be a valid assessment, because none is properly focused to measure just what the teacher intends to measure: the aspect of the benchmark relating to the functions of state government. It's true that students who have acquired this knowledge might display it in any of the assessment formats listed, but students who do not have the knowledge might also complete any of these activities successfully. A touchstone question to ask about any activity or assignment used for assessment is "Would doing well on this assignment demonstrate that the student has mastered the intended objective?" In this particular example, the answer is "not necessarily."

What kind of assessment would be an appropriate format? What activity would provide students with the opportunity to demonstrate their ability to identify the primary functions of state government? Here are a number of valid possibilities:

- Working from memory, students could display the functions of state government in a chart or booklet.
- Students could sort a list of governmental functions into categories of local, state, and federal responsibilities. (Note that this activity requires

students to use only the recognition type of memory; the first option in this list requires students to produce remembered knowledge.)

- Students could assemble a collection of newspaper articles that relate to state government in action, with every student getting a copy of every article. Then, using this collection for reference, students could explain what governmental function each story addresses.

- In answers to written test questions, students could describe the functions of state government.

Students who can complete these assignments independently and successfully would be demonstrating their mastery of that part of the state standard. The key point to note is that each of these valid assessments focuses students on the functions of state governments, whereas the assessments in the invalid list are wide open and allow students to focus on any aspect of their field trip. Each assessment in the invalid list could be modified to require students to demonstrate understanding of the benchmark information. Try your hand at this: go back to the list of invalid assessments, and tighten the focus of each so that it requires students to "identify the primary functions of state governments."

Another question the instructional designer must ask is "Would doing well on this assessment be sufficient evidence that the student has mastered the objective or standard?" In the post–field trip example, any one of the valid assessment tasks could measure some or all of the "state" part of the required achievement. An objective that requires students to "explain the causes and consequences of the collision of cultures in Middle America" might require several assessments focused on the individual steps of learning and another one focused on students' mastery of the big, integrated picture of these events. On the other hand, one assessment may serve to measure mastery of more than one objective. High school students writing a children's book about the American Revolution might be demonstrating their achievement of several objectives for content knowledge, as well as an objective for the ability to write for a particular audience. One way or another, a teacher must find out when and to what degree each objective has been mastered by each student.

Objectives and Assessments May Be Expressed in Identical Statements

Leaving a gap between objectives and assessments is a common problem, but sometimes it's the lack of a gap—objectives and assessments stated in exactly the same language—that can be confusing to novice instructional designers. It raises the question of what the difference between objective and descriptions of assessments really is. Both focus on student learning outcomes, so why say the same thing twice?

The difference between an objective and an assessment, whether or not they are stated in the same terms, is their purposes. To put it another way, the difference is in the way that the teacher uses them.

Here, for example, is an objective that could absolutely double as an assessment description:

> *Students will write a paragraph in Spanish incorporating the 10 new vocabulary words in today's lesson.*

In this example, when the teacher is clear about the objective of writing a paragraph that demonstrates comprehension of 10 new vocabulary words, she is thinking about students' demonstrating their progress toward that goal as they go through the lesson (via formative, in-class assessment of defining new words, identifying objects or actions in pictures, creating practice sentences, etc.). The objective describes the goal toward which everyone in the room is working—teacher and students—and that goal is an activity that the students will engage in at the end of the lesson, at which point the goal becomes the assessment. During the lesson, the thinking and skill application inherent in the paragraph writing is the objective. At the end of the lesson, when learning has been accomplished, the thinking and skill application serves as the assessment.

Only some objectives and assessments can be expressed in identical statements. It's up to the teacher to examine these single statements for validity as an objective and then again for validity as an assessment. This requires you to pay close attention.

Would this objective, for example, be valid both as an objective and as an assessment?

Students will label continents and oceans on a world map.

We'll walk through this one together. The teacher writing this objective decided that the way to have her students demonstrate the learning she wants them to acquire by the end of a lesson—knowledge of the names and locations of the world's continents and oceans—will be to label this information on a map. Having decided that students will demonstrate their learning through this activity, the teacher must now pin down all the details of the activity to ensure that it's truly an assessment of student learning rather than just a learning activity.

Return to the touchstone question for gauging an activity's validity as an assessment: "Would doing well on this assignment demonstrate that the student has mastered the objective?" When we visualize students doing this work, we again have to answer "not necessarily," because the activity, as described, is not specific enough. What if students simply copied continent and ocean names from a labeled world map posted in the front of the room? If they did that, doing well on the assignment would demonstrate their ability to copy information in that situation, not their mastery of the names of continents and oceans. They will have achieved the letter but not the spirit of the objective. The teacher needs to close the gaps between her objective and her assessment by visualizing her students at work and making the assessment statement more specific:

Students will label continents and oceans on a blank map,
working independently

or

Students will label continents and oceans on a blank map as part of a written test.

The Practical Details

In this discussion of assessments, we are really working with two levels of assessment design. The first level is the description of the assessment that goes into the lesson plan. As you've seen, this description must show the alignment with objectives and identify the format in which students will demonstrate their thinking and learning. It is usually a single sentence.

At the second level, the teacher must work out the practical details of assessment tasks. These details are not necessarily addressed at the time that the original plan is created, and if they are, they may need some revision when the time for assessment comes around.

Establish Expectations for Student Performance

Although Chapter 8's discussion of rubrics and scoring guides will explore this topic in greater detail, it's important to note here that expectations for student performance must be worked out in advance of any assignment that's used for assessment. For illustration, let's return to some of the objectives that we examined in earlier chapters:

Students will identify images in a poem.

In this objective, the verb, *identify,* conveys the intellectual work students will do. They'll be required to look at words and phrases and determine which ones describe images. First, the teacher must decide what format the assessment task will take. Here are some possibilities:

- On a written test, students could read a poem and underline the images.

• Students could create a poster or booklet to be used by next year's students that explains and identifies images in particular poems.

• Students could read a poem projected or written on the board, make note of one or more of the images it contains, and draw what the images bring to mind.

• In a journal entry, students could explain what literary images are and produce examples from texts, from memory, or from imagination. (This task allows students who are ready to engage in higher-level thinking to do so. It makes explicit the principle of Bloom's taxonomy that lower levels of thinking are embedded in the higher levels: they must be able to *identify* a term and *explain* it before they can *produce* examples and use their understanding to *create* images of their own.)

In clarifying expectations for student performance, the teacher must select the poems that students will use in their identification of imagery. Because all the assessment tasks considered involve the student working independently, the selected poems must be at a level of difficulty that allows every student in the class to work independently. The teacher must also decide how to handle specific elements associated with the chosen assessment task. If the teacher asks students to translate a poem's images from words to graphics, will the teacher allow all students to also provide a written explanation of the graphics they produce?

When you are working to clarify your expectations, keep asking yourself what course of action will best support the student's achievement of the objective. If we extend Mager's Hey Dad test from objectives to assessments, we see that the products of any of these activities could be taken from the classroom to show an outside evaluator evidence of students' achievement of the objective. These products could also be used as learning activities or for the purpose of diagnostic, formative, or summative assessment.

Here's another example of an assessment description focused on measuring students' ability to use knowledge of imagery:

Students will create a poem that includes imagery.

"Create a poem" establishes both the level of thinking required (Synthesis/Create) and the format in which that thinking will be demonstrated. The teacher's next step is to decide what constitutes an acceptable poem and provide students with that information before they start creating. A rubric or checklist (see Chapter 8) is a good way to do this, but any clear communication about what the teacher requires is acceptable.

Teachers sometimes tire of students' questions about assignment details, but students' experience with grades has trained them to be careful of exercising their own choice and judgment. They will want to know such things as required length and topic of poem, number of images, how many of the five senses should be used, and whether rhyme is required. If a single image about any school-appropriate topic will do the job (inspired by Sandburg's fog-as-a-cat, for example), students need to know that. In designing this assessment, the teacher will need to decide which variables will be factored into the grade and which can be left up to the students. This information is generally what students want when they ask, "How long? How detailed? What are you looking for?"

If the teacher's objectives and requirements are clear to students, many of them will stop asking questions. They will know the point and the parameters of the assignment when the teacher says something like, "The purpose of this assignment is primarily for you to show that you understand how to use literary imagery. I also want you to have the chance to be creative and express yourselves, but if you clearly demonstrate that you can create three images that fit into a single poem, you will be successful in this assignment. The checklist tells you what the basic requirements are; the other decisions about your poem are up to you."

As the teacher thinks through the details of this assessment, he might add a requirement that students explain in writing how the images they chose contribute to the poem. This information would give him additional insight into the students' understanding of imagery and alert him to misunderstandings—perhaps a student who thought she was using imagery when in fact she was using some other literary device. In that case, the lesson objectives would be

> *Students will create a poem that includes at least three images.*

> *Students will explain how the images contribute to the poem.*

The two corresponding assessments would be

> *Students will create a poem that includes at least three images.*

> *Students will write an explanation of the contributions these images make to the poem.*

Note the close alignment between objectives and assessments. Note, too, that once the teacher has written these objectives and their aligned assessments, the learning activities (see Chapter 9) that students will need to engage in become obvious: they will need to practice identifying images, analyzing images' contributions to poems, and writing and analyzing images in their own poems.

Assess Every Learning Objective

An objective without an effective assessment is, for at least some students, the equivalent of having no objective at all.

Consider a real-world example: my objective is to lower my cholesterol level from 240 to 200 or lower. I can follow my doctor's advice (healthy eating, exercise, weight loss), and by tracking what I eat, keeping an exercise log, and monitoring my weight, I may think I'm measuring progress toward that goal. But unless I assess my progress by tracking my cholesterol level, the functional objective I'm working toward really is a healthier lifestyle instead of lower cholesterol. I might assume that the result of my activities will be the lower cholesterol I want, but without measuring that cholesterol level, my doctor and I don't know what progress I'm actually making and, thus, if I should be doing something else, such as taking medication. I am not seriously working toward my objective if I don't check to see whether I am achieving it.

In school, objectives exist to establish what students will learn. If we do not assess our objectives, our students' learning—and, critically, their failure to learn—is invisible, just as my cholesterol level is invisible unless I have it measured. If we don't measure student mastery of the objective, it doesn't matter what the objective says or even whether it's there. If the teacher is satisfied with merely exposing students to new information, that is the teacher's functional objective, but that is not the same as student learning.

An old saying tells us that "what gets rewarded is what gets done" or "what gets measured is what gets done." This is a useful reminder for teachers: make sure your assessments measure and reward the kind of learning that is required.

For beginning instructional designers coming to understand how to teach and assess standards-based skills and knowledge, it's wise to think of lesson plans as documents that describe desired outcomes and ways of achieving those outcomes. In this context, a lesson plan should ensure the correspondence between objectives and assessments—that all objectives are assessed and all assessments are aligned with objectives. If a teacher establishes objectives but decides not to assess the students' achievement of them, that teacher should have a sound reason for the decision and be fully aware that some students will probably not achieve the objective. Possibly none will, and without assessment, the teacher will never know.

Like all rules, however, the rule of "assess every objective" has a few exceptions. Objectives do not need to be formally assessed if

- They are affective objectives, aimed at changing students' values, attitudes, or social behavior.
- They are connected with learning goals that are not part of state standards.

Of course, a teacher is always free to assess either of these kinds of objectives if so inclined, and if time permits, and most teachers will probably be gathering informal assessment data just by watching and listening to students during instruction. It the outcome is important to you, assess it.

Create Assessment Materials

Careful planning of an assessment will reveal the materials that you and your students will need—and they are usually more detailed and numerous than is obvious. At a minimum, assessment tasks will probably require you to create one or more of the following documents, depending on the format of assessment you choose.

Instructions (aka "the assignment sheet")

Students should not have to rely solely on a teacher's oral instructions when embarking on any assessment beyond the most simple. Putting main points on the chalkboard is a big help, but in the case of complicated assessment activities, students should receive written instructions—assignment sheets that describe the work students will be undertaking and how it will be assessed.

Writing instructions is a good way for a teacher to see all the decisions that must be made about the assignment: length, purpose, degree of student choice, and criteria for evaluation (often a rubric). You may decide that showing students a model of a complicated project is the best way of ensuring that they understand what learning you expect them to demonstrate and how you expect them to demonstrate it.

Checklist or rubric

Discussed in Chapter 8, a checklist or rubric is an integral part of the assessment document set.

Test (aka "the assessment instrument")

If your assessment is a traditional one—a written test, for example—you need to put the document together or choose an existing test document before you design the associated learning activities. Make absolutely sure that the test measures student achievement of valid objectives and what you will be teaching. Whatever skills or knowledge you expect students to demonstrate on the test should be covered and practiced as part of your instruction.

PRACTICE EXERCISE: Developing Assessments

Examine the following objectives, and develop assessment statements for them. In each case, begin by imagining what a successful learner could do to demonstrate achievement of the objective. That will require you to think about the students' thinking and about the format of the assessment. Decide, also, whether the assessment task you design will be formative or summative. The first one has been done for you.

1. Objective: *Students will explain why governments sometimes restrict trade with other nations.* Assessment statement: *Students will create a skit or newscast explaining some social and economic forces that lead governments to restrict trade with other nations.* (Formative assessment)

2. Objective: *Students will contrast the conductivity of copper and carbon.*

3. Objective: *Students will classify foods according to their places in the food pyramid.*

4. Objective: *Students will analyze the causes of conflicts that arise between their peers.*

Now revisit the objectives that you wrote for the last chapter, translating from the common core standards (see pp. 98–102). Imagine what students who have mastered those objectives will be able to do, and create one or more assessments built on their new skills and knowledge.

Evaluating Assessment Design

The most reliable and valid evaluation of an instructional design comes from students' responses to it, with their learning being its ultimate test. However, it is important to make all design elements as strong as possible before subjecting students to them. As you review your chosen assessment tasks, test them against the following strengths and common mistakes.

Strengths: The Qualities of a Strong Assessment

There are seven qualities every assessment must have—and three more that are highly desirable, if not always feasible.

It is closely aligned with objectives and, by extension, academic standards.

Embedded in this alignment is a statement of the thinking and learning students will demonstrate.

It includes instructions.

A clear set of instructions, including clearly worded test questions, will ensure students know what is expected of them.

It has validity.

A strong assessment assesses what it is supposed to assess. The way to ensure the validity of an assessment is to close any gap between it and its objective(s).

It has reliability.

The kinds of students for whom it is designed will reliably show their level of learning using this format year to year, class to class. This quality cannot be determined until the assessment has been used with different student groups, but as you use certain assessment formats repeatedly, check for reliability. If some students who have achieved the objectives cannot perform the assessment successfully, it is not a reliable assessment.

It has a clear audience.

A good assessment is designed to convey information to a particular audience. This may be the teacher and the individual student, or other students (when work is posted, or the assessment is a performance of some kind). The audience may be parents, administrators, or the community at large. Be aware that even if you consider the audience to be only yourself, your grading of the assessment may be discussed among students and with parents after you return it to your students.

It has a clear purpose.

A good assessment has a clear and specific aim. Is it to get a snapshot of students' understanding of today's lesson? To allow students to express their creativity? To help them explore ways in which their lives are affected by the topic being studied? Is it to pull details together into a big picture? Is it to show the teacher whether the students are ready to move on? Is it to show the students what they do and do not know? Visualizing a successful learner using and demonstrating skills and knowledge can help you see what you want the assessment to measure.

It is achievable.

A good assessment is one that students can complete—on both practical and intellectual levels. This sounds obvious, but beginning teachers have been known to under- or overestimate the demands that some assessment tasks place on students. If the task requires specialized materials and resources, such as background knowledge, time, or creativity, that some students do not have (for example, "make a political cartoon tonight"), it will not be a valid assessment of student learning. Instead, it will assess their willingness to cooperate or their access to resources.

There are three additional qualities that are desirable but not always reasonable for every assessment:

It integrates factual information, understanding, and intellectual skills.

The easiest assessments to design and grade are those that measure students' memory of facts. Such assessments have a place, but in K–12 classrooms, no teacher should limit assessments to tests of this kind. Students should also be developing an understanding of concepts and of how individual facts are part of a larger picture. They need opportunities to demonstrate their understanding of the importance of facts and ideas as well as their memory of them. Students should also be developing intellectual skills, such as the ability to read, write, solve problems, use their imagination, and communicate clearly. Generally speaking, assessments that help students learn and motivate them best are those that integrate understanding, intellectual skills, and factual information because this combination allows students to express their mastery of the course content in ways that are meaningful to them.

It incorporates some student choice.

Students usually value opportunities to show what they know and can do (even if they complain about the assignment when it's given), and different students will be successful at demonstrating their mastery in different ways. Teachers whose instructional goals are clear in their own minds can often afford to be flexible about ways in which students demonstrate their learning: they can give students choices of assessment, such as writing, drawing, composing a song, and so on. Sometimes it is in the students' best interest to show their learning in a particular format, and in many cases a particular format is part of the disciplinary knowledge, such as writing out answers to math problems in a certain way. Even so, students often can be given choices: which problems in a set to do or which method of problem solving to use. Successful teachers know that students are more likely to feel committed to the whole idea of learning if teachers allow them to shape the learning experience to fit their own needs and preferences wherever appropriate. After all, it is the student's education and future at stake, not the teacher's.

It furthers students' opportunity to take ownership of their learning.

Feedback should come not only from teachers, but also from other students and from the learners themselves. Of course the teacher takes responsibility for assessing each student's learning. However, it is natural for human beings to care about the opinions of their peers, and teachers can use students' social interests to further their academic growth. Giving students opportunities to work together and to provide instruction, feedback, and suggestions for one another can be motivating for all concerned and helps create a classroom community that takes learning seriously.

Students can also be involved in creating assessments. They can write quiz questions, suggest assessment formats, and collaborate with the teacher in establishing grading criteria. Ultimately, we hope that all students will learn to evaluate their own work and take responsibility for their own learning, but they will need practice and guidance in developing this ability. The art of teaching includes knowing when to step in to give information and direction, and when to get out of the learner's way. If we keep in mind that students should become independent learners, then we can allow ourselves to relinquish a degree of control when appropriate.

Just as learning goals—instructional objectives—must be meaningful, worthwhile, and, when achieved, useful to the learner in some present or future way, assessments should be meaningful activities that allow the student to demonstrate worthwhile learning.

A Mistake Rooted in Education Philosophy: Assessing Content That Has Not Been Taught

Almost everyone who has ever been a student has faced an assessment task that raised the question "When did we learn that?" or even the outraged complaint, "We never learned that! This isn't fair!"

Assessing content that hasn't been taught may be a careless mistake, but it is more often a mistake of a more philosophical bent—a deliberate decision made for sincere if, in my viewpoint, misguided reasons. Let's look at some of the justifications given for assessing content that is not taught and analyze the effect on student learning.

Justification #1: The need for differentiating "challenge" questions

A teacher might argue, "I need to include questions that will separate the *A* students from the rest of the pack." This argument, based a certain philosophy of education, generally leads to the inclusion of questions about minor material that was mentioned only once, perhaps indirectly, or questions that require students to do significant independent analysis, synthesis, and evaluation under test conditions. The teacher may challenge the students to identify and discuss themes in a novel or in history without having previously taught them how to identify and understand theme. The teacher may challenge the students to produce insights (also not explained in class) into a scientific principle or to apply mathematical concepts to new kinds of problems.

This practice is based on a model of teaching that sorts students into a normal-distribution curve rather than on a model that does everything possible to help all students become proficient in a standards-based curriculum. When higher-level thinking skills are to be assessed, they should be taught and practiced beforehand. When details are important enough for students to learn and use, those details and the reasons for their importance should be highlighted during lessons. Outstanding students should be recognized and rewarded for their gifts and achievement in ways that do not put other students at an unfair disadvantage.

Testing students on content you haven't taught can be legitimate if you're certain that they've received instruction on this content elsewhere. However, teachers should be ready to meet students where they are (rather than where it is assumed they should be) and provide instruction from there. If you want students to make presentations to the rest of the class, for example, find out whether they know how to do this before you go ahead with the assignment. If they have never been taught how to speak in public, manage visual aids, take turns presenting within a group, and practice sufficiently before presenting, then you must instruct them and give them practice before you grade them on their performances. If you choose to skip instruction on some aspect of an assignment, either make sure students have an alternative source of information and guidance (perhaps a librarian or a school writing center, for example) or grade students only on those aspects of the assignment that you know they have been taught. You can grade students on content, for example, and give feedback on public-speaking performance with the understanding that when students have had adequate practice, the performance will be graded as well as the content.

Justification #2: The need for students to teach themselves

Here, a teacher might say, "I've introduced the idea; now it's up to the students to teach themselves." This argument basically contends that not every new idea and skill that students need to learn must be followed up with focused learning activities.

There is no universal agreement on how much responsibility for learning lies with the student and how much lies with the teacher. However, a focus on successful student learning means finding out how much support for learning students need and receive outside the classroom. Some parents supervise homework; others do not. Some students have quiet home environments conducive to homework and study; others do not. Some students have time set aside daily for homework; others hold jobs and care for younger siblings when they are not in school. Teachers must make realistic decisions about how much class time to spend practicing skills and reviewing information before their students are ready for a formal assessment or evaluation. Informal assessments, in which teachers ask students to tell them what they know or demonstrate their progress, should be occurring every day.

Justification #3: The need to defeat memorization

"I need to keep assessment content a surprise; otherwise, students will just memorize a small set of facts and learn nothing else." This argument may come from a benevolent place: the teacher's concern that students will focus on getting *A*s but have no breadth or depth of knowledge about the subject. There can also be a related concern that with everyone knowing exactly what to memorize, everyone will get high scores, and grade inflation will result.

What's important to grasp is that this feared outcome—this shallow learning—is likely only if there are weaknesses in the design and execution of teaching and learning, like objectives that do not require depth and breadth of knowledge or objectives that are valid but misaligned with their assessments. Limited learning might also result from inadequate instruction, despite the presence of objectives and assessments that are sound. For example, if a teacher presents content in the form of a lecture, film, or reading assignment and does not provide students with sufficient guided opportunity to make sense of the material, then students may well have achieve little depth and breadth of knowledge. But when instruction covers a topic fully and students are supported in learning what the teacher wants them to learn, it will be obvious to the students what the test will require of them, and most will focus their attention on learning that material.

Students should not have to guess what the teacher considers important for them to learn. As novices in the discipline, they generally do not know what experts consider to be vital information as opposed to detail. If the teacher's focus is on successful student learning, the teacher will make students aware of what they should know and not let them waste time memorizing information that is not relevant to their understanding of the important concepts. Making sure students know what is important is consistent with telling them what the instructional objectives of a lesson are and with telling they why they are studying what they are studying and why they are doing what they are doing. Keeping students in the instructional loop in this way improves motivation and cooperation, as students see the teacher as helping them learn rather than trying to trick them into failing.

When preparing for tests, students should know the range of information they are expected to learn and what level of detail they are expected to memorize—dates, names, events, concepts, vocabulary, and so on. If they will be expected to synthesize information about causes and effects, for example, or to discuss a theme (imperialism, energy, induction and deduction), they should know that before the test. They should also be told what kind of test they are studying for—multiple choice, essay, short answer, oral quiz, something else? They should know whether they will be expected to explain or define in their own words, develop a concept at length, or recognize a correct answer among several possibilities. What they prepare for is what they will learn. If they feel hopeless about preparing because they have no idea what to expect, they may give up on preparing altogether.

This does *not* mean, however, that a teacher who decides to use a traditional test has to tell the students beforehand exactly what questions they will be asked. It is reasonable to expect the students to know more about a topic than one test will measure, so the test questions will sample the students' knowledge.

The message of this section, in short, is that assessments are opportunities for learners to demonstrate their learning, not opportunities for teachers to play "gotcha!" When test questions ask about material that students have had an opportunity to investigate, make sense of, and practice working with—and if the test questions are clearly worded—most students should be able to answer most of the questions correctly. If they do not, the teacher and the students need to investigate the reasons.

Five More Mistakes in Assessment Design

The typical errors in assessment design are likely to be the result of falling back on traditional classroom habits and not thinking carefully about how the assessment will support students' learning of standards-based objectives.

As you read about the following common mistakes, think about why they are not consistent with achieving the best student learning possible. I have provided my explanation for the first two.

• *Treating a learning activity as an assessment.* Since learning activities often look much like assessments (many activities may be used for both), the teacher must think carefully about the conditions under which students perform the task. Learning activities require that students have support for learning: access to information, guidance from the teacher, help from peers, and so forth. Assessments require students to demonstrate knowledge individually. Even if the objective is for students to work together, each person must demonstrate the ability to do that, and so must be assessed as an individual working with others. If an assessment task is divided among a group of students, or if it is done with students having access to the information that it is intended to assess, they may appear to do well without actually knowing what they are supposed to know. Although students may like having learning activities treated as evidence that they have achieved learning outcomes, this practice denies them a real education. When designing assessments, teachers can avoid this problem by keeping an outside evaluator such as a principal or parent in mind. As students leave the classroom, can each and every one demonstrate all the required skill and knowledge?

- *Using assessment as punishment.* Since many students dread tests (because they fear that they haven't learned what the teacher expects them to learn, or because studying and answering test questions are unwelcome labor), it seems natural to use quizzes or tests as punishment or as a threat of punishment to control behavior. However, using any aspect of learning as punishment teaches students to dislike the subject and perhaps to dislike all learning. If we remain focused on successful education, we will manage behavior in ways that do not erode students' willingness to engage with academic content.

Now try explaining why the following assessment practices do not support student learning:

- *Using the same assessment format all or most of the time.*
- *Factoring personal preferences into the grading of assessment assignments.* An example would be requiring a certain kind of ink and paper.
- *Evaluating students on their execution of the format rather than on their demonstration of content knowledge.* This is seen, for example, when students' public-speaking skills, creativity, artistic talent, popularity, humor, or great storytelling affect their evaluation.

The next chapter continues our look at assessment with an examination of checklists and rubrics.

8

Checklists and Rubrics

Assessment should contribute to students' learning by requiring them to explain, apply, analyze, synthesize, and be creative with new knowledge. In addition, assessment requires teachers to give feedback that helps students continue to fine-tune, deepen, and broaden their understandings and their skills. Checklists and rubrics are tools that can help to clarify the assessment task and the feedback associated with it.

Checklists

A *checklist* is a tool students can use to make sure they have met all requirements of an assignment that will be assessed. The teacher creating the checklist decides which features of the assignment are important enough to factor into how the work will be graded or otherwise evaluated. As Figure 8.1 shows, although a checklist allows a student or the teacher to note whether the key requirements of the assignment have been successfully completed, this format does not generally provide a place for elaboration, further evaluation, or extensive comments. However, when it comes to creating a checklist for your own assignments, the format is up to you. Your task is to create a feedback form that allows you and your students to communicate effectively about the important goals of the assignment.

Figure 8.1 • A Standard Checklist

Checklist for "My Favorite Folklore Character" Essay	Student Check	Teacher Check
1. Essay explains at least three reasons for choosing the character in adequate detail.		
2. Introduction to the essay draws the reader in and provides context.		
3. Conclusion leaves the reader with an image or idea that pulls the whole essay together.		
4. Standard English is used throughout.		
5. Essay has an appropriate title.		
6. Essay is written neatly in ink.		

A *grading checklist* is a checklist with space for the teacher (and the student, if you so desire) to assign a grade or some other kind of evaluative indicator. The grading on these checklists almost always takes one (or more) of four forms: (1) a symbol, such as a letter or check mark, (2) points, (3) narrative comments, or (4) standards-based reporting, which is expressed as something like "advanced, proficient, basic, below basic" or as numbers from 1 to 4 representing those levels of achievement. Standards-based evaluations focus on how well the student is mastering academic standards and are not intended to include other factors that commonly influence grades, such as comparison with other students, effort, cooperation, and so on.

The checklist in Figure 8.1 could be modified to capture information about grading in one or more of these forms, as shown in Figure 8.2. This figure also illustrates how checklists may include a space for student comment. Students prompted to comment on their work can provide additional insight about their thinking and their experience with the assessment assignment. In this example, a student might say, "I had trouble coming up with the third reason, and I think that two reasons would have been enough." As the teacher, you might go on to rethink why you asked for three reasons. Could the learning objectives be met if the students were told to provide between two and four reasons? It would certainly give students more choice and control over their work. Another student might say, "The conclusion was easy because we practiced with little kids' stories" or "I still get confused about how to spell *then* and *than*."

Figure 8.2 • A Grading Checklist

Checklist for "My Favorite Folklore Character" Essay	Student Comment	Teacher Grade
1. Essay explains at least three reasons for choosing the character in adequate detail: *30 points*		
2. Introduction to the essay draws the reader in and provides context: *15 points*		
3. Conclusion leaves the reader with an image or idea that pulls the whole essay together: *15 points*		
4. Standard English is used throughout: *20 points*		
5. All requirements on assignment sheet were followed: *20 points*		
Total number of points out of 100:		

Note in Figure 8.2 that the points are allocated to emphasize the features that the teacher considers the most important. This emphasis can be communicated in other ways, as well. You might, as illustrated in Figure 8.3, add a "Weight" column, in which you note a factor by which the points assigned to each element will be multiplied. If you make all the elements worth a standard number of points (10, as in the figure, or any number you choose), you can easily adjust the overall proportion.

Figure 8.3 • A Grading Checklist with a Weighted Points System

Checklist for "My Favorite Folklore Character" Essay (10 Points Each)	Student Comment	Teacher Grade	Weight
1. Essay explains at least three reasons for choosing the character in adequate detail.			× 3
2. Introduction to the essay draws the reader in and provides context.			× 1.5
3. Conclusion leaves the reader with an image or idea that pulls the whole essay together.			× 1.5
4. Standard English is used throughout.			× 2
5. All requirements on assignment sheet were followed.			× 2
Total points:			

All instructional materials you hand out to students should be designed and proofread with care, but assignment sheets, checklists, and rubrics must also be tested against individual students' imagined performances. When creating these materials, think about how students will use them and how your grading will be shaped by them. Try out possible point ranges to see how much flexibility you need. The greater number of points you use, the more choices you will have when it comes to providing students with information about the quality of their work. If you use 1, 2, or 3 points, you have a simpler but coarser system than if you give yourself the option of assigning more—let's say 30. Students who receive 2 points in the 1–2–3 system may receive anywhere from 10 to 20 points, or 1 to 4 points, or other variations (depending on how you decide to divide up the range) in the 30-point system. Take another look at Figure 8.2, and consider the difference if you simplified the point system in that checklist to add up to a total of 20 points instead of 100. This would result in the following point allocations:

1. Essay explains at least three reasons for choosing the character are explained in adequate detail: 6 points (not 30).

2. Introduction to the essay draws reader in and provides context: 3 points (not 15).

3. Conclusion leaves the reader with an image or idea that pulls the whole essay together: 3 points (not 15).

4. Standard English is used throughout: 4 points (not 20).

5. All requirements on assignment sheet were followed: 4 points (not 20).

The most obvious difference is that the essay is now worth 20 points instead of 100. But other changes may result, so try out different point possibilities on imagined or actual student work. One consequence that you will notice is that the simpler systems group students into larger groups—all students will be in the 1's, the 2's, or the 3's, which means that more students will be receiving the same grade. When you look at those in the 2's, for example, are you satisfied with having all of those individuals receive the same evaluation score? In the systems that use more possible points, you may have only three students (or none) receiving the full 30 (or 50, or 100) points, while other students' scores are spread out over the whole range. Do you find that different point systems favor students in the top, middle, or low achievement rankings? Only you can know what will work best for you and your students on a given assignment.

Rubrics

A *rubric* is a specialized type of checklist. Like other checklists, it tells students what a completed assignment or finished product should include, but it also contains information about how the teacher will determine a student's score, grade, or level of mastery. There are two main types of rubrics: analytic and holistic. Analytic rubrics are the most common and often the most useful for shaping student learning.

The example in Figure 8.4, a rubric for the same "My Favorite Folklore Character" essay assignment, gives the teacher flexibility in grading within each category. When using it, the teacher would write the number of points awarded in each box and then add them up to arrive at the final point total, which would serve as the student's grade. A simpler rubric would eliminate this flexibility so that the "Advanced" ranking, for example, would award 3 points for each element; the "Proficient" would award 2 points; the "Basic," 1 point; and the "Below Basic," zero points. When using that rubric, the teacher would simply circle the appropriate box. In either case, however, this rubric gives all elements the same weight. If you want to assign more weight to some elements than to others, change the format.

In Figure 8.4, the "Below Basic" category does not have a set point value. Having the option of giving some points to students who attempted to meet the requirements but who didn't achieve a basic level allows you to show them how close they were to achieving a passing score. Keep in mind that if you are working in a school that uses letter grades, for this assignment you will need to inform students of both their grades and their level of achievement. Alternatively, you could replace the ratings at the tops of the columns with letter grades, so that "Superior" becomes "*A*," and so on down the line.

This example also illustrates the importance of conducting imagined practice runs of the mathematical system your rubric sets up. Here, the points for a passing score can range from a high of 50 to the lowest of the "Basic" range, 15. Scores on rubrics are usually divided by the number of

Figure 8.4 • A Standard Rubric

Advanced 9–10 points	Proficient 6–8 points	Basic 3–5 points	Below Basic 0–2 points
Essay explains at least three reasons for choosing the character in.adequate detail.	Essay explains two reasons for choosing the character in adequate detail.	Essay gives and explains only one reason, or the explanations for two or more reasons are inadequate.	Essay gives no reasons or provides no explanation.
Introduction to the essay draws the reader in and provides context for the argument to follow.	Introduction lacks either a strong draw or clear explanation of what the essay will address.	Introduction lacks either a draw or an explanation; if both are present, they are weak.	Introduction is absent or too weak to function as it should.
Conclusion leaves the reader with an image or idea that effectively pulls the whole essay together.	Conclusion has a weak or undeveloped image or idea with potential to pull the whole essay together.	Conclusion simply repeats what has been said in the essay.	Conclusion is absent or too weak to function as it should.
Standard English is used throughout.	There are a few nonstandard uses of punctuation, vocabulary, and sentence structure.	There are numerous nonstandard uses of punctuation, vocabulary, and sentence structure.	There are so many nonstandard uses of punctuation, vocabulary, and sentence structure that the essay is difficult to read.
All requirements on assignment sheet were followed correctly.	Some requirements were not followed.	Some requirements were not followed or most were not followed correctly.	Requirements were not followed or were followed incorrectly.

Total points: _____   Achievement level: _____   Grade: _____

categories (here, it's 5) to find the average (here, between 3 and 10). If you like, you may also adjust the number of total points possible to reflect the importance of the assignment in relation to other assignments. You could make this essay worth 100 points by adding a zero to everyone's score so that the final range would be from 30 to 100.

Before you give any grading tool to students, you must know what you will do with the various possible results. If a student earns perfect scores on all aspects of the folklore character essay other than the "Standard English" category, which hovers between a 2 and a 3, will that student earn a "Proficient" rating overall? Are any of the categories in the rubric too important to be just one of five grading criteria? These decisions are part of a teacher's job. The guiding question, as always, is "What will best support the learning that students need to do?"

Never forget that a rubric quantifies the importance of each element in students' eyes, so if you allot 20 percent of the grade to spelling and 20 percent to content, students will see spelling and content as having equal importance. Assigning weight to each element is another reminder to limit the number of elements included, since a rubric with 15 elements will necessarily provide a small weight to most or all of them. Rubrics lay out the degrees of success possible for a given assignment, showing which qualities receive full credit and which receive diminishing percentages of that credit. But a rubric can also address "all or nothing" behaviors. For example, cleaning up after a lab activity might be graded on the basis of whether it is done satisfactorily (5 points) or not (0 points), which saves the teacher the time it might take to describe and quantify gradations of cleanliness. The lab station is either clean or it isn't; a student can earn full points or no points at all.

Some rubrics reflect a decision to grade an assignment on a very small number of elements. For example, an art teacher may grade a painting assignment on technical use of the materials and overall aesthetics. Within these categories, the teacher will list the most important elements: color, shading, shapes, and composition. Some possible features will be omitted in favor of focusing students' attention on the most important ones, but the subcategories make the rubric a much more useful teaching and grading tool than it would be if the students were told simply that their work would be graded on technique and aesthetic appearance. If the students do not need any more information than that, they probably don't need a rubric at all.

About Holistic Rubrics

The rubric example in Figure 8.4 is an *analytic rubric,* which means that it shows a breakdown of the whole folklore essay into component elements. Most rubrics are analytic rubrics. A *holistic rubric,* by contrast, describes the whole product or performance. It allows the assessor to consider all features of the student's work together and assign the work a single rating. This is useful and appropriate in some situations. For example, when your expectations for a product or performance can be summed up in just a few words, a holistic rubric like the one shown for homework, below, can provide feedback that is appropriately brief.

Well Done	Partially Well Done	Not Well Done
Assignment is complete, accurate, and legible.	Assignment is at least 50% complete [*or whatever portion you want to give credit for*]. Work is mostly accurate. Work is legible. [*Will you give credit for illegible work?*]	Assignment is less than half done *or* Most work is inaccurate *or* Most work is illegible.

Recording students' performances on routine tasks like homework can be done with points, checks, pluses and minuses, or grades. Similar brief evaluations can use frequency scales ("Always," "Sometimes," "Never") or intensity scales ("Very," "Somewhat," "Not at All"). You might decide to give yourself the flexibility to record intermediate levels of performance for a student who, for example, never quite earns the top rating but sometimes comes very close—or comes very close to earning the lowest rating. The question you need to answer when considering a short holistic rubric is "Is it productive to look quickly at a student's work and put it into one of [your number] categories?"

As you can see, making decisions about where to draw the lines about something as apparently straightforward as doing homework can become complicated. In addition to keeping your objectives in mind as you make these decisions, keep observing your students to see how they are using your system. Is it encouraging them to do better or more work, or are they manipulating it, or are they just giving up?

In holistic assessments, no aspect of the performance or product counts as nothing, because everything about it contributes to the whole. Holistic rubrics are appropriate for complex performances such as those in the arts, which includes many types of writing. Many states have a rubric for essays available to all teachers that list content, organization, language use, and conventions of standard English. Some include other elements, such as sentence fluency; some list details within each category. Many of these rubrics are holistic even though they mention individual elements because they are formatted by overall achievement, usually in three, four, or five levels. The holistic format gives the evaluator the flexibility to weight elements as appropriate to the individual case. For example, a student writer who makes some spelling errors and a couple of factual misrepresentations could still earn the highest rating for the essay because the ideas and their expression are so beautifully handled.

What Kind of Rubric to Use?

When you are deciding whether to use an analytic or a holistic rubric, consider which kind of feedback would be most instructive to your students and which kind of evaluation is most appropriate for the product or performance you are assigning. Consider, too, the option of including a holistic element in an analytic rubric, such as "Overall, the work shows understanding of concepts." Holistic rubrics generally include some analysis of the qualities that make a product strong or weak; these are listed in a brief description of each level.

The distinction between analytic and holistic rubrics is not sharp. The difference between the two is that an analytic rubric requires the teacher to note achievement on the specific elements listed, whereas a holistic rubric requires the teacher to consider the work as a whole. Generally speaking, an analytic rubric is most helpful when students are learning parts of a whole, whereas a holistic rubric tells them how well they have performed in a genre they already understand.

The Benefits of Using Checklists and Rubrics

These assessment tools help students see what skills and knowledge they should employ. Students should be trained to use rubrics as if they were going to grade assignments themselves, because they should use them that way either informally (checking to make sure they have met all the criteria) or formally (actually giving their work a grade and justifying it in writing). Teaching students how to use a checklist or rubric to its fullest advantage teaches them to become more independent in assessing their own learning and abilities. Eventually, students will internalize the accepted criteria for various kinds of products—essays, posters, lab reports, solutions to math problems—and rubrics will no longer be necessary. However, K–12 schooling is the place for students to learn those criteria; rubrics help students learn about forms of these genres.

In addition to informing students what they should be attending to in performing the assessment task, rubrics help teachers grade more fairly and efficiently. The rubric helps a teacher attend to all the listed elements in a student's work, rather than be distracted by one or two particularly wonderful or dismal features. If, for example, a student's report shows a serious misunderstanding of the content, the teacher can either give no credit on that part of the rubric or, if the work is simply unacceptable, hand it back to the student for revision. In either case, the teacher can see that this student is in need of more instruction, practice, and feedback in the content but can also note that other features of essay writing may or may not be at such a low level.

Efficiency in grading comes from knowing what you are looking for in students' work, particularly when you have decided that you are not going to try to include every detail. The layout of the rubric can help you avoid having to write the same comments on many papers, since you can circle or highlight the words in the rubric that apply to each one. Efficiency in grading diminishes as the number of elements increases, however, so when you are deciding what to include, keep your own available grading time in mind. This is particularly important when you are using a rubric to grade public speaking, since you will probably be making decisions about each student's performance in the few minutes that the student is performing. The longer the list of elements you are grading on, the more complicated your task will be. Possibly the feedback to each student will be less reliable with a long list, since you won't have time to think about each point when there are many of them.

Potential Challenges in Using Checklists and Rubrics

An Internet search for "rubrics" or "grading checklist" will yield many more sites than any one person can visit. Many of these sites allow a user to create rubrics and checklists for specific tasks in specific disciplines, including those for children too young to read. These kinds of sites can be very helpful, but it is a mistake to use a grading tool that you have not scrutinized—and probably modified—to make sure it matches your objectives, your assignment, and your students.

What to Include

Checklists and analytic rubrics force teachers to either limit the number of features that will influence the evaluation of the product or describe the features in terms broad enough to encompass many component features.

If you keep the descriptions broad ("Conventions of standard English are followed," for example), you give yourself room to grade punctuation, spelling, syntax, grammar, verb tenses, capitals, and anything else in this category. However, broad descriptions provide students with minimal guidance in using these conventions correctly, and if you decide instead to add the subheadings of "Punctuation," "Spelling," and "Pronouns," you will focus their attention on those elements. The choices you make depend on your objectives. The important point in making decisions about the rubric is that what you put on the rubric is what students will pay attention to. And what you put on the rubric is what you are committed to using as the basis for evaluating the work.

Some elements of an assignment do not belong on a rubric because they are too important to be just one of several graded skills. Safety in a lab is one example: a student who is not following safe practices should not simply lose a percentage of points for lab work and get a *B* instead of an *A*. That student will probably need to be removed from the lab if the infraction is at all serious. Similarly, if you decide that your students need an audience participation grade for a guest speaker, rudeness ought to result in more than a deduction of points.

Students "Managing" Their Effort

Rubrics can work against a teacher's ideal of every student doing his or her best. With all students able to see how a "Proficient" performance differs from a "Basic" performance, there is a risk that some will use the rubric as an instruction sheet for how to cut corners and get a passing grade with the least amount of effort. However, looked at from another point of view, if the points are allotted judiciously, a rubric can encourage such students to do what is most important. As you fine-tune the language of a rubric, keep all of your students in mind—those who want to excel, those who want only to pass, and those with varying ability levels. Try imagining how each will use the rubric.

A teacher who hands out a rubric or checklist commits to using it fairly. Make sure that your rubric does not allow students to earn a passing grade even if they completely miss one category, such as content knowledge—unless that is all right with you because the objectives of the assignment are not primarily concerned with content knowledge but with (for example) working productively with peers.

Matching Performance Descriptions with Actual Performances

Generally speaking, the easiest student performances to describe are those at the top and bottom of the achievement scale. Trouble may come with describing work that is flawed but still meets some level of achievement. There are so many ways that a student's work can be successful and flawed simultaneously that one rubric can never include all the possibilities. Consider the rubric excerpt here:

Advanced	Proficient	Basic	Below Basic
Explanation is thorough, supported with details and facts.	Explanation is incomplete, partially supported with details and facts.	Explanation is brief, minimally supported with details and facts.	No comprehensible explanation; no details or facts related to the concept are present.

Imagine that a student of yours has written an elegantly brief, complete explanation that makes his or her understanding clear but has mentioned only one supporting fact—which happens to be the most significant one. Imagine another student who has written a lengthy explanation that includes many details and facts, only some of which actually support the central concept. Imagine a third student who has written some facts related to the concept but has not explained it. Which of these boxes will you circle when you are grading these students?

These questions have no easy answers, but asking yourself how well each person is demonstrating achievement of the objectives can help you make the necessary decisions. These problems can be minimized by paying close attention to the wording when creating the rubric: an "Advanced" explanation could be brief, for example, if the student has a gift for concision. Instead of describing the "Basic" explanation as *brief,* describe what really matters, which is how complete and correct an explanation is. Students who try to cover all bases by mentioning everything they can remember from the unit of study are not necessarily demonstrating understanding, so in the "Advanced" category, a more useful description might be "Explanation is thorough and accurate, well supported with relevant facts." Are "details" different from "facts" in this context? You can decide whether you need to include both in your rubric descriptions. Your objectives should help you write a rubric (as well as use it) if you visualize successful learners using their new knowledge. Sometimes, working on the wording of a rubric leads to the realization that a checklist like this would be more useful:

Criteria	Student's Comments	Teacher's Comments & Grade
Explanation is complete and accurate, showing understanding of the concept.		
Explanation is well supported with relevant facts; no unrelated details are included.		

This checklist example also demonstrates the advantage of keeping criteria separated. When you combine two or more criteria in a single cell, you have to decide what to do when a student has mastered one and failed at the other. In this case, the separation of explanation from its support by data would allow you and the student to note whether each has been successful.

Effective Communication and Design

Because you are creating the rubric or checklist to facilitate communication with your students about their learning, you can be innovative in your design. Here are a couple of ways that you can modify standard formats to accomplish this goal.

The first option is to keep one cell of the rubric blank so that you can write in it whatever is most appropriate for the student. You can assign any number of points or grade percentage to this open cell and use it to focus the student's attention on what you think is most important about the student's work. For example, you might say, "Excellent improvement in organization over previous reports" or "Every paragraph has at least two run-on sentences, so see me if you don't understand how to correct this problem."

Another innovative possibility is to require students to respond to your comments either in a conference or in writing (perhaps on the back of the rubric or in a journal entry). Students may not understand or agree with a teacher's evaluation of their work, and when they don't, they rarely have an opportunity to let the teacher know unless they initiate it. But their confusion or disagreement provides a golden "teachable moment." Even when students are pleased with your evaluation, you can gain important insights into their thinking when they respond to your evaluations.

What to Do with the Data

Checklists and rubrics for particular assignments sometimes include items that are not part of the instructional objectives and not directly part of the final product. Here are some examples:

- "Used class time well."
- "Participated in group brainstorming session."
- "Took notes in class discussions."

- "Used peer feedback to revise."
- "Worked to the best of his or her ability."

A student could produce an outstanding product without doing any of these things, just as a student who diligently did all of them could produce a weak product. Although an examination of the many controversies about grading is beyond the scope of this book, an analysis of assessment requires that the assessor consider carefully what will be done with the results of the assessment. In schools, results are usually expressed in grades. In a standards-based system, educators must make difficult decisions about what grades are based on, and particularly whether they should be significantly influenced by a student's level of cooperation. If a checklist or rubric emphasizes the classroom behavior that a teacher wants rather than content knowledge, everyone (teachers, students, parents, administrators) should be clear on that point, and everyone should understand the implications for student learning. When a student's *B* in math is based on an *A* in compliance with the teacher's rules and a *C* in content learning, everyone involved should know this is the case. When compliance is embedded in a rubric that appears to be about learning, the message to students and parents may be muddled.

As you work with checklists and rubrics, experiment with separating content knowledge from all the other criteria that you value, including requirements for the materials and format of the project. This could result in seeing that some students master the content but do not use the learning processes (e.g., group work, taking notes) that the teacher sets up and express their mastery in formats and materials that are different from those the teacher has requested. And the opposite could be true with a student who follows orders but doesn't learn well. What grades are appropriate?

This brief mention of grades is intended only to point out that teachers have many decisions to make and questions to answer as they develop assessment tasks and grade them. Examine assumptions, and keep your sights on student learning.

PRACTICE EXERCISE: Creating a Checklist or Rubric

1. Examine the objective and assessment pairs that you wrote at the end of Chapter 7, and choose one as a practice subject for creating a checklist or rubric. If you want guidance, take these steps:

— Visualize the successful learner accomplishing the assessment task. What is that student doing that shows you that the objective has been attained?

— List what you are noticing about your imagined student. Look for content knowledge, kinds of thinking, and performance of skills. It may help to imagine another student who isn't as far along in mastering the objective. What do you see in your mind's eye about the differences between these two students? This difference can help you pin down important features of the successful learner's performance. It can also help you see shortcomings in performance that you want room to comment on.

2. Once you have identified performance elements directly aligned with a standard, consider other requirements of the assignment. (Creating a rubric or checklist can help you evaluate the assignment, because it may reveal gaps or weaknesses in the design of the assessment task, such as unnecessary demands in how the task is carried out. However, do include elements of the assignment that will influence the grade because they are important for students to know and do, such as inclusion of research findings. You may create a checklist for assignment requirements and a rubric for evaluation of learning.)

3. After you have identified all the important features of the student's performance that will be the basis of evaluation, organize them into a format that distributes the grading weight appropriately. Leave openings for comments to individual students, if you desire.

4. Test your rubric or checklist by imagining how you will evaluate various students:

— The student who has mastered the objective and performed the assessment task to your specifications.

— The student who has mastered the objective but did not perform the assessment task as you required, perhaps because of a lack of certain skills or materials.

— The student who may know a good part of the required content but who cut corners in performing the assessment task to the degree that you cannot gauge the student's level of knowledge.

— The student who tried hard to follow your directions to the letter but who hasn't understood the content.

This review of rubrics completes our work on student learning outcomes. You know what they are, what they reveal about the teacher's job, and how to establish and evaluate them. In the next chapter, we will see how teachers can use learning outcomes as the basis for designing classroom learning activities.

9

Designing Learning Activities

We have finally arrived at the point where the curtain rises and the class-room action begins. Learning activities are the public face of instruction, a visible performance of learning and teaching. They are what engage students in taking in new information, thinking about it, making meaning of it, and using it in various ways. Learning activities are what students notice about teaching, what they remember about learning, and what they see themselves directing when they embark on a teaching career. What is not so well known about learning activities is that they depend on solid objectives for their relevance and utility. Without alignment with a foundation of objectives, learning activities don't make sense; they don't add up to anything coherent at the end of the semester.

As we saw in Chapter 7, a teacher developing an assessment uses an objective whole, so to speak, figuring out what someone who has achieved the whole objective could do with that knowledge. Because both objectives and assessment describe an end point in the learning process, the teacher's imagination can be focused on that one point. By contrast, when designing learning activities, a teacher must focus on a process—a series of steps and changes that lead students from not knowing to knowing.

Designing learning activities requires teachers to break down the process of thinking into stages. Once we understand objectives and assessments, we can state, for example, that at the end of the lesson

Students will analyze uses of fact and opinion

and that they will demonstrate one application of this skill in an aligned assessment:

Students will write an analysis of an advertisement's use of facts and opinions

but how are they to get from not knowing anything about this intellectual work to actually being able to do it?

Background Knowledge for Lesson Designers

Two kinds of background knowledge are tremendously helpful when planning instruction: (1) insight into what stimulates the brain to think and learn, and (2) an understanding of the thinking skills articulated in Bloom's taxonomy.

Natural Ways of Learning

We are born knowing how to learn, but our natural ways of learning are not always included in schooling. Traditionally, much of our natural behavior has not been seen as compatible with institutional efficiency and maintaining the structures of classrooms. An instructional designer must be aware of "natural ways of learning" and look for opportunities to incorporate them into the institution of school. I recommend considering the following general truths:

• Human beings are social. Of course there is a wide range of social behavior among individuals, but generally speaking, people are stimulated by interacting with others. Part of being social is expressing oneself, which most people enjoy.

• Human beings use language to think as well as to communicate. Many individuals find that rephrasing new explanations or information in their own words helps them learn it. When language and social interests are combined, we find learners talking to one another about their new understandings or reading what they have written to one another.

• Human beings generally learn best when they understand the purpose for learning. Sometimes the "why" of learning can also be connected to our social and linguistic natures, as when we prepare a performance or product to be shown to others or for others to use.

• Human beings enjoy moving about (especially young human beings).

• Human beings enjoy solving problems and puzzles.

• Human beings enjoy discovering things.

• Human beings enjoy being creative and making things.

• Human beings enjoy meeting a challenge successfully.

• Human beings enjoy competition and public performance (degrees of enjoyment will vary from one person to the next, and high levels of it are associated with high levels of self-confidence).

• Human beings enjoy humor and the unexpected.

• Human beings enjoy telling and hearing stories.

• Human beings enjoy learning how their world works.

With this list fresh in your mind, consider some learning formats that are widely used in schools. How does each link to or fit in with natural human characteristics?

• Cooperative learning
• Making presentations
• Peer feedback
• Brainstorming, pair-sharing
• Discussion

- Making posters and creating booklets and drawings
- Writing songs
- Putting on skits
- Discovery learning
- Playing games and engaging in contests and competitions
- Hands-on learning using manipulatives, props, other materials; lab experiments
- Simulations
- Authentic projects that engage students with the world outside of school
- Field trips
- Problem solving

Consider, too, some other common formats for learning that do not draw on these natural human qualities: prolonged lecture, prolonged note taking, individual seatwork, or any other format that requires students to be immobilized, solitary, and silent for long periods, and which requires them to stay focused on a subject in which they have little interest.

Thinking about natural learning will help you find ways to keep your students alert and engaged. As we work through the planning of the lesson on fact and opinion, look for opportunities to incorporate the physical, social, and intellectual activities that human beings enjoy.

Bloom's Taxonomy

In addition to drawing on natural learning, instructional designers can use Bloom's (1956) taxonomy as a kind of map for getting students from one level of knowledge to the level that characterizes mastery of the objective. Bloom contended that any level of thinking encompasses the levels below it, so when the objective is to have students working at the level of Analysis, for example, we can turn to the simpler kinds of thinking that Bloom described and use them as stepping stones to take students where they need to go.

In this chapter's discussion, we will work from the revised Bloom's tax-onomy (Anderson et al., 2001), the first two levels of which are Remembering and Comprehending/Understanding. "Remembering," in this context, means that the student has elemental familiarity with the material, can recognize it, and can recall something about it. "Understanding" means that the student can give examples, summarize information about the topic, and express its meaning in his or her own words.

Say our goal is to design learning activities for the objective "Students will analyze uses of fact and opinion." In this case, thinking at the Under-standing/Comprehending level would entail identifying simple examples of facts and opinions, generating characteristics of facts and opinions, and per-haps generating some tools to distinguish between expressions of fact and of opinion. Perhaps students might assemble a list of common expressions that are associated with opinions—personal statements such as "I think" and judgments such as "the best," "the worst," "wonderful," and "disgrace-ful." Other words that commonly appear in opinion statements are "always" and "never." These identifiers are not foolproof indicators of opinions, so we would also want students to learn to recognize them as such—as suggestive, as reasons to probe more deeply. We would also want students learn that facts can be verified (a process that itself can involve opinions, but this is a level of ambiguity that some students might not be ready to deal with).

As students work with examples and show that they can explain what facts and opinions are and how to tell the difference, we might expect many of them to proceed to the next level of thinking, which would involve apply-ing this new understanding. At the Applying level, students can carry out a procedure, although they may not know exactly why the procedure works to get the desired results. In the case of this lesson, students might begin to apply their understanding of facts and opinions to the question the objec-tive addresses: "How can facts and opinions be used?"

The fourth level of the revised Bloom's taxonomy, Analyzing, is fre-quently intermixed with the third, Applying. Thinking at these levels can involve deciding how or when to apply a rule or procedure and deciding how to interpret the results of application activities. Fortunately, it doesn't matter that there is no sharp division between levels of thinking; what's important is that we acknowledge that there are levels and that we teach at least to the highest level the objective requires. It's fine to give students opportunities to work at higher levels as long as you are sure that these higher-level assignments support students' achievement of the objective without putting unnecessary stress on them.

In the case of this lesson, analysis is the highest level of thinking necessary to achieve the objective. It's likely students will quickly learn to separate obvious examples of facts and opinions—a skill that requires only recognition of a few characteristics. However, when arguments are expressed more subtly, and when statements contain mixtures of fact and opinion, students will need to break them apart—analyze them—so they can organize the ideas into those that are supported by real-world evidence and those that are generated by emotion or values. Some ideas will not fall clearly into one category or the other.

Let's remind ourselves of the assessment established for this objective. It requires students (1) to analyze an advertisement in order to locate the facts and the opinions it contains, and (2) to identify the contributions that each fact or opinion makes to the ad's effectiveness. The difficulty of the task will depend on the subtlety of the persuasion in the ad and on how much students know about the facts related to the product being advertised. This is a situation that illustrates why a teacher's knowledge of exactly what the assessment task will require of students is important in designing learning activities. Preparing students to analyze one kind of advertisement can be very different from preparing them to analyze another.

Armed with knowledge about how people learn—through activities that draw on natural functioning and through graduated levels of thinking—the instructional designer is now ready to begin designing the learning activities.

Step 1: Plan How to Start Students' Thinking

Any time you ask students to take in new information, you should first stimulate their thinking about what they already know. The term for this is "activating background knowledge." Background knowledge comes from a wide range of sources, both in school and out, and it has a profound effect on what learners can make sense of and what they cannot. Decisions about how to activate background knowledge will be heavily influenced by who your students are.

Let's examine some ways to activate the background knowledge related to the telling-fact-from-opinion objective and its assessment. First, it's a good bet that virtually all students will have had extensive exposure to and experience with advertisements, but we need to find out what they already know about fact and opinion. Here are some possible ways to activate their background knowledge:

1. Begin class with a provocative statement, oral or written (e.g., "It's a fact that the Harry Potter movies are the best movies ever made"). Get the students talking about fact and opinion, and write these terms on the board. Then find out what the class can brainstorm about the characteristics of each.

2. Write, "This class has 25 students in it" and "This class is the most interesting class in the school" on the board. Ask students what's fundamentally different about these two statements.

3. Give some (or all) students large strips of paper with facts or opinions written on them, and ask that they post them on the board under a heading of "Fact" or "Opinion." Or do this by means of a handout: students can organize facts and opinions written on the handout, on cards, or on slips of paper, using the handout as the organizing frame. They can work alone or consult with a partner.

4. Stimulate discussion with a video or print example of facts and opinions, such as a movie clip, a cartoon, or an excerpt of a magazine or newspaper article. A headline could be enough.

5. If your students are old enough and knowledgeable enough to handle it, use a controversial statement that some people believe to be factual and some believe to be opinion. This activity begins the lesson at a more sophisticated level, as it assumes that students already have a solid understanding of undisputed facts and how to distinguish them from opinions.

6. Find a situation that your students are likely to know about, perhaps a story in the news, a court case, a community event, a school conflict, a comic strip, or even an argument that you invent. Ask students to identify some facts and opinions in what the participants are saying.

Any of these activities would get students thinking about the subject of a lesson and could also provide us with a window into what they already know about it. The next step is to plan a way for them to learn more.

Step 2: Plan How to Provide Access to New Information

It is obvious that learners need access to the information they are expected to learn. But it is easy for a novice teacher to make the mistake of providing inadequate or irrelevant information and inadequate access.

One common problem for many students facing new information is that they do not, in fact, have the background knowledge they need to make sense of it (see Reeves, 2004). If you deliver information in the form of a reading, lecture, or video that students do not understand because they lack the vocabulary or other essential background knowledge, they will effectively lack access to that information. They will be unable to "unlock" that text. When you review the sources of information you're considering, try imaginatively experiencing them as your students would. Look at the sources through the eyes of the average student, the gifted student, and the disengaged or underprepared student. What are the access points? Where are the potential roadblocks? How might you navigate around these barriers?

The most familiar way to present information is through an expert-centered format, such as a lecture, reading, or video. Alternatively, you may choose to set up an opportunity for discovery learning—a chance for students to discover information on their own. (Consider the natural human preferences involved in discovery: finding things out, solving problems, working and talking with others, being active, and meeting a challenge.) Discovery can be set up as a big project that takes days of class time, or it can be as simple as asking students to categorize elements of a topic instead of telling them what belongs where or asking them to examine an artifact such as a slave narrative or a feather and telling them to figure out the purposes for its existence and how it achieves those purposes. Once students have invested some time and thought in figuring something out, they are more likely to be interested in learning "the answer."

Discovery learning is also consistent with a good general rule for all teachers: "Don't do any work that students can do themselves." As you plan activities, keep asking yourself which parts of it the students can do. This is particularly important when you are choosing how they will access new information. Yes, the simplest path is to just tell them what you want them to know, and sometimes that *is* the best way to get the information across. But unless the telling is brief and on point, many listeners will mentally drift away. Notice that "listening to teacher talk" is not on the list of natural human satisfactions.

Step 3: Plan How to Help Students Connect New Information to Established Learning

"Meeting" new information in the form of a reading, lecture, or video or through discovery is only one step in learning. Students may understand the information and may close their notebooks at the end of this exposure feeling that they've learned it. However, unless they mentally connect this new material to other information they have learned well, chances are good that a few weeks later, only traces of the new information will remain in their minds. Consider, for example, what you remember of a movie that you saw or a book you read a year ago—one you neither loved nor hated but would rate as fine or OK. You might be able to remember what it was about, but can you summarize the plot in more than a sentence or name more than two or three characters? The same is likely to be true of people you met only once and of informational programs you watched on TV. A famous story about Euclid, the great Greek mathematician, tells of his teaching geometry to King Ptolemy of Egypt. The king apparently grew tired of spending time on practice exercises and asked for a faster, simpler way to learn. Euclid is said to have replied, "Sire, there is no Royal Road to learning." It was true then, and it's still true, for kings and for everyone else.

Learners need opportunities to concentrate on the important features of new information. They need to work with it by rephrasing or reformatting it, applying it, comparing and contrasting it with other information, and forming connections with related material or with personal associations. Ideally, they will have a chance to be creative with it. You can consult Bloom's taxonomy for inspiration on how to do this. Keep the objective and the assessment task in mind as you choose ways for students to make something meaningful and lasting of new learning.

The chart in Figure 9.1 shows one way to keep the various factors organized. Begin with the assessment task, and then choose one of the levels of Bloom's taxonomy to work with—all the way from the first level (Remembering) to whatever level the assessment and objective require (or higher, if that will help students learn). Then either select a few natural human behaviors and build the activity on them, or design the activity and then see what natural proclivities it entails. You can keep tinkering with the details until you are satisfied that the learning activity will help your students achieve the objective and accomplish the assessment task in ways that are stimulating and engaging to them. The figure shows two examples.

Figure 9.1 • Activity Examples Linked to Bloom's Taxonomy
and Natural Ways of Learning

Objective: Students will analyze uses of fact and opinion. Assessment Task: Write an analysis of how fact and opinion are used in an advertisement.		
Thinking Skills	What Students Will Do	Natural Ways of Learning
Analyzing (contrasting fact and opinion)	Distinguish between fact and opinion in a film clip of a courtroom scene; discuss in small groups.	• Social: Watch people interact. • Problem solving: Figure out what is fact and what is opinion. • Discussion. • Discovery: People can make opinions sound like facts and vice versa.
Creating	Create a skit or comic strip in which someone is trying to persuade others to do something *or* provide dialogue for people in a picture.	• Be creative. • Social: Work with others to create and present the skit/comic strip/dialogue to rest of the class. • Use humor, if appropriate. • Tell a kind of story.

At any point you think would be beneficial, prompt students to consolidate and preserve their new understanding by writing or drawing or acting. Each of these activities requires them to make personal meaning of the new material—to use their creativity to produce something unique. Or, if students have been working in small groups, pull the class together and have them consolidate learning by writing it on the board.

Step 4: Plan How to Monitor Student Performance and Give Feedback

Learning activities are wonderful opportunities for teaching. Although the fundamental idea behind a learning activity is that it will provide students with what they need to pursue learning—the means to "teach themselves" and one another by carrying out the work that's been designed for them to do—learning activities also give the teacher time to work selectively with individuals, alone or in groups, to help them master what they need to master, as they need to master it. This is sometimes called "chair-side teaching," and it is an essential part of teaching practice. It is also a way to differentiate instruction.

As you plan learning activities, visualize yourself finding out what each student is doing and thinking while working on each activity. Think of yourself circulating through the classroom, looking over shoulders, listening, and asking questions and deciding whether to give feedback and what kind of feedback to give. You will be continuously evaluating each student's progress toward the objective and his or her success in completing the assessment task. You do not need to interrupt students who are working well; a nonverbal sign of approval such as a smile or pat on the shoulder can let the student know you are happy with the work without breaking the student's concentration. If a group is engaged in discussion, you might pull up a chair and listen in for a minute or two (checking around the room frequently to let other students know they're still being monitored), but you do not have to join in their conversation just because you are there. Sometimes your attentive presence provides all the stimulation and reassurance learners need.

Each activity you design will have its own relationship to the objectives of the lesson; it will provide students with opportunities to work on part or all of the learning described in the objectives. When you are clear about what each learning activity provides, you will know what you are looking for as you monitor students' work. Practice and experience make it much easier to see what students are thinking and learning as they talk, write, draw, or create in other ways.

A Pause for Illustration: Sample Activities for the Fact and Opinion Lesson

Let's pick up the design of this lesson at the point at which students will begin to apply their developing understanding of facts and opinions. We know that students can identify clear statements of facts ("George Washington died in 1799") and opinion ("Popsicles on a hot day are the best!"). But before students will be ready to perform the assessment task, they will need to practice identifying facts and opinions in advertisements and analyzing their contributions to the advertisement's effectiveness. If time allows, we'd like them to apply this practice to other media and situations as well, as this will strengthen their skills by broadening the contexts in which they know how to use them.

The most straightforward way for a teacher to teach skills is by following this pattern:

1. Model (demonstrate) the task.
2. Go through a version of the task a second time with the whole class participating and contributing.
3. Require students to perform the task with a partner.
4. Require independent performance of the task.

If the task is complex, more demonstrations and more supported practice will be necessary. If it is not, students may be ready to perform independently right after the demonstration.

This pattern is widely followed and is a useful part of a teacher's repertoire of learning activities. However, we might be able to make it more interesting through our choice of materials or variations in the process. Thinking about natural ways that people learn reminds us that they enjoy stories in which people do something adventurous, dramatic, heroic, or comical. So examples that we choose for this lesson could be clips from ads on TV or print ads that show a scene from an implied story. Or we could vary this pattern by asking students to do some modeling themselves—after the class has worked on examples, of course, so that we could see who is ready to demonstrate.

If the class includes students who like to perform, another idea would be to give pairs or groups of three a simple script—or situation from which they create a script—in which they act out a situation that reveals facts and opinions in characters' interactions. Any situation in which people are choosing a course of action or trying to persuade one another will do, such as arguing, solving a problem, making a decision, or interpreting what they see or otherwise experience. A child might be trying to persuade a parent to increase an allowance or a teacher to banish homework. A person might be criticizing another's behavior . . . the possibilities are endless.

In designing ways for your students to learn, you will be well advised to have more practice activities and materials available that you expect to need. This will give you the flexibility of choosing, in the moment, the one that seems most appropriate for your students' learning needs and the mood of the class that day. What you don't use for one class might just be the perfect fit for another.

Students' work on these activities will show you when they are ready to perform the assessment successfully. They should have practice in all the skills that the assessment requires. (In working toward our example objective, they should practice analyzing the ways that advertisements use facts and opinions and practice putting the results of their analysis into their own words, perhaps orally first, and then in writing.) They should get peer feedback as well as teacher feedback on their work so that the assessment task is not a jump into the unknown, but instead a demonstration of skills and knowledge that the students themselves know that they have mastered.

Figure 9.2 summarizes some learning activities that could help students learn to "write an analysis of an advertisement's use of facts and opinions." They are ordered as they might appear in a lesson plan.

Using a chart like this can help ensure you keep learning activities aligned with the assessment task and with students' natural behavior. This

Figure 9.2 • Learning Activities for the Fact and Opinion Objective

Objective: Students will analyze uses of fact and opinion.		
Assessment Task: Write an analysis of how fact and opinion are used in an advertisement.		
Thinking Skills	**What Students Will Do**	**Natural Ways of Learning**
Remembering	Choose something they like (e.g., something to do, read, eat, watch, play), and write a sentence describing how they feel about it. Then write another sentence giving a reason that they like it. (Example: Eating a raspberry popsicle on a hot day is awesome. I like it because the popsicle is sweet and cools me off.) Examine their statements for opinions and underline them in a wavy line. Then find facts and underline them with a straight line. Discuss with partner to check for accuracy. Write facts and opinions on the board under headings.	• Self-expression • Imagination • Communication • Discovery: Facts that support an opinion • Performance (a minor one): Think of something that will interest peers.
Analyzing (contrasting fact and opinion)	Distinguish between fact and opinion in a film clip of an argument between two people; take notes during the clip and then discuss in groups of three. As a whole class, list facts and opinions on the board.	• Social interaction: Watch people interact. • Problem solving: Figure out what is fact, what is opinion • Discussion • Discovery: People can think their opinions are facts and others' facts are "just their opinion."

Thinking Skills	What Students Will Do	Natural Ways of Learning
Analyzing	Distinguish between fact and opinion in an advertisement. Explain the roles that facts and opinions play in persuading people to buy the product. Use a handout to record this information. Then discuss findings with the other two people in the class who worked on the same advertisement. Afterward, the group explains findings to the whole class.	• Problem solving • Self-expression • Discussion • Performance • Creative interpretation: Explain why the ad is effective.
Creating	Using the writing about a favorite thing or activity, sketch plans for a print or TV ad. Use both fact and opinion. Write an explanation of why specific facts and opinions were chosen to influence consumers. Get peer feedback in groups of four.	• Creative expression • Social interaction: Work with others to improve the ad. • Use of humor, if appropriate • Storytelling

format cannot capture every detail or decision a teacher must make about setting up and directing the activities, and it is certainly not a complete lesson plan (see Chapter 10). However, it could include an example of our next topic, the final step in designing learning activities, planning for closure.

Step 5: Plan for Closure

"Closure" is a learning activity, but it is often separated on a lesson plan from other learning activities because it has a character and purpose all its own. At the end of a lesson, students benefit from reflecting on their new learning—stepping back to think about how the activities they engaged in fit together to create an understanding of new concepts or to clarify familiar ones (such as "fact" and "opinion"). Closure provides an opportunity for students to connect their new learning to previous learning, maybe even in another subject, or to look ahead to projects they have heard they will do (such as create their own ad campaign for a book or a presidential candidate).

Closure may take any form that allows students to do this kind of reflecting and synthesizing. It may be as simple as a discussion about how facts and opinions in ads influence their effectiveness. It may be a writing assignment in which students "free write" about the new content and what it brings to their minds, or it could be a structured activity that requires students to make connections. Whatever form closure takes, however, it does not introduce new material. The point is to have students think about material already learned. It also does not involve the teacher doing the thinking or talking or writing; the students are actively doing these things while the teacher guides, listens, and observes.

From a teacher's point of view, closure is a great opportunity for formative assessment. As students talk and write (and maybe draw, sing, or act) about their understandings of the new content, the teacher gets to see the results of the learning activities. It is also a great opportunity to see what kinds of differentiation will need to be done as individual students express different understandings. Through observing students at work on classroom activities—particularly during closure, when students are expressing comprehension of the whole lesson in their own words—teachers can see specifically who needs further support to attain this knowledge. More generally, they can see what kinds of support will benefit this or that student now and in the future. When a student reveals, for example, poor comprehension of a reading, poor recall of new terms, or uncertainty about how to apply new skills, these difficulties are likely to reappear in other lessons.

Additional Advice for Designing Effective Learning Activities

The lesson on fact and opinion we have looked at is relatively straightforward. It does not require students to learn a great body of content and then grapple with some version of the big question "What does it all mean?" Distinguishing fact from opinion requires mastery of a concept rather than of a body of knowledge. As such, this lesson offers many opportunities for examining real-world examples that students are already familiar with. In content-heavy learning, as when students are required to learn large amounts of new information about history, literature, science, or math, their teachers may find it more challenging to make learning activities interesting. Here is some advice:

• *Keep students active and doing as much of the work of the class as possible.* Set them up to discover and solve and do the tasks that keep the lesson running, such as drawing a name from a hat or writing on the board. At moments during the lesson (and when you are reflecting on your teaching afterward), ask yourself, "Who is doing the thinking and talking here? Who is actively doing the work?"

• *Look for ways students might apply something about the new content to themselves so that they can incorporate it into their personal spheres of experience.* For example, if you are teaching about the planets, have students contrast the experiences of living on Earth (gravity, temperature, atmosphere, seasons, length of day and year, water, life-forms) to the experience of being on another planet or in another location on our planet.

• *Use as many natural human ways of operating as possible, as often as possible.* If you are requiring students to summarize a reading, for example, see if you can at some point incorporate social interaction—or creative illustration of the content or making a story out of it or connecting it to some current happening in the world beyond school.

• *Choose formats that will be interesting to use.* Not so long ago, students were excited by the opportunity to use computers, and in the 1840s, students were probably excited by new books and chalkboards. Now they may enjoy using new technology, but other formats can be interesting even if they're not new, such as fitting pieces together to make a whole, building something, or using unexpected or unconventional materials—food, for example—to illustrate a concept.

• *Make sure that the learning activity is purposeful.* It will be if you have aligned it with the objectives and upcoming assessments. Make sure that students understand the purpose, as well. They might be inclined, for example, to regard a journal reflection or drawing exercise as mere busywork, but if you explain how these activities help them process new information and express their learning, students are more likely to take this work seriously and use it to accomplish that purpose.

PRACTICE EXERCISE: Designing Learning Activities

Continue your work on your plan for your students' learning by reviewing the objective, assessment, and rubric or checklist that you have written. Describe some or all of the learning activities your students will need in order to achieve the objective, being sure to

1. Align the activities with the objective and assessment to the learning goal in sight.
2. Incorporate appropriate levels of thinking, working up from the Remember level (or wherever the students begin this lesson) to whatever level the assessment requires.
3. Provide opportunities for students to access new information.
4. Provide opportunities for students to use natural learning methods.

5. Provide opportunities for students to practice the skills that the assessment requires.

6. Provide closure.

In the following (and final) chapter, we will examine some formats for lesson plans. You are ready to put all the work you have done so far into a solid, useful, and interesting plan for your students' learning.

10

Creating Plans for Learning

If you have completed the practice exercises in the previous chapters, you have the foundation of a plan for your students' learning. You have created the weight-bearing elements, so to speak, that will become a full plan when you add the information about what you and your students will do—the topic explained in this chapter.

A great deal of information for teachers about lesson planning is available through books, articles, other educators, and the Internet. You can find lesson plans, unit plans, ideas for activities, reports from teachers about resources, and assessment options. A beginning teacher might be very tempted to take shortcuts by adopting a ready-made lesson plan, adding or substituting an activity from another source, adopting an assessment from yet another source, and then feeling prepared to teach. This is an understandable temptation, especially when these materials are supplied by reputable sources, such as state education departments or professional organizations. The problem with this approach is not that these lesson plans or activities are poorly developed (although the quality does vary widely); the problem is that adopting a plan without working through one's own understanding of how it leads to appropriate student learning is like saying, "I'm ready to perform in this play because I have the script right here. All I have to do is say the lines I'm supposed to say." Every good actor is doing much more than speaking lines; every good teacher is doing much more than shepherding students through an activity and an assessment task.

Just as an actor must understand the character he is playing from the inside out and in the context of the whole play, so a teacher must understand the content from the inside out and in the context of the whole curriculum. An actor must do everything possible to provide the audience with a full experience of the drama—characters, action, conflict, outcome, connection to issues larger than the individual characters. A teacher must do everything possible to provide each student with a full experience of the ideas in the lesson. Teachers have the additional responsibilities of matching their teaching to the individual needs of their audience and checking that audience for evidence that the goals of the event were achieved.

Terminology Matters

Before we begin the work of putting together the components that previous chapters have addressed, let's examine the term "lesson plan." This widely used and familiar term originates from a teacher's point of view: a lesson plan is the teacher's plan for carrying out a lesson. It implies learning, but repeats the error of assuming that if learners go through Activity X, they will learn Content Y. Of course, it's true that if the lesson is planned and delivered by a teacher who knows how to use every part of it to generate appropriate learning, the term used to describe the plan will not matter a bit. However, a consistent focus on students' *learning* rather than on teacher performance shows us that a more accurate description of what we are creating when we design instruction is a "plan for student learning." The difference, again, is that "lesson plan" is a plan for a lesson that may or may not result in student learning, while "plan for student learning" says directly that learning is the focus and the goal. The shift in perspective embedded in these terms is the goal of this book, so in the rest of this chapter the terms "plan for student learning" and "student learning plan" will replace "lesson plan."

The Elements of a Student Learning Plan

Learning plan formats vary in terminology, layout, and emphasis, but they must all include answers to these two questions: "What will students learn?" and "How will they show their learning?" By now, you will recognize that these questions address objectives and their assessments. Everything else that goes into planning and teaching is in the service of students' success on the assessment, which is how we know that they have achieved the objective. This includes the question of which learning activities they will engage in. When you have internalized what students will learn and how they will show their learning, you will understand how to work with just about any legitimate learning plan format.

Having identified these essentials, what remains can be understood in terms of what other contribution it makes to the process of teaching and learning a standards-based curriculum. For example, well-known educator Madeline Hunter recommended seven elements that are not necessarily required for every lesson but which have been shown to positively affect learning (Hunter, 1982; Hunter & Russell, 1994). Notably, instructional objectives are not among these elements, because Hunter identified them as essential (not optional!); objectives must be in place before the activities of a lesson could even be considered. Today, many learning plans include some or all of Hunter's seven elements:

1. Determining the kind of access students will have to new information
2. Modeling desired thinking and skills
3. Checking for understanding
4. Guiding students' practice
5. Providing independent practice
6. Communicating to students what the objective is
7. Starting a lesson by creating an anticipatory set

Three of these elements—checking for understanding, guided practice, and independent practice—can support formative assessment efforts. Hunter's inclusion of formative assessment in the learning activities is a good reminder that formative assessment tasks usually double as learning activities. Remember, anything students do that shows them and the teacher what they understand can be used as assessment.

Another important point about Hunter's seven elements is that they are presented the in the order Hunter believed a teacher should consider them, the reason being that "each element is derived from and has a relationship to previous elements" (Hunter & Russell, 1994, p. 89). This is why that the beginning of the lesson, creating the "anticipatory set," is last on the list, although it frequently appears first on contemporary renderings of Hunter's ideas. ("Anticipatory set" is a psychological term describing a state of mind that is focused on, and ready to respond to, something coming up. The introduction to a lesson is the way the teacher generates that state of mind in the students.)

In addition to Hunter's seven elements, many learning plans include some variant of an overarching question that the lesson will address. Generally, these questions are known as topical, guiding, or essential questions.

Topical questions address the topic of the lesson directly by putting the content of the objective into a question that the lesson will answer. For example, if the objective is "Students will explain how transportation systems have developed," the topical question is "How have transportation systems developed?"

Guiding questions, also known as *essential questions,* extend our thinking into the world beyond the classroom. They connect the curriculum to larger areas of human experience, provoking thought and exploration of the complexities of an issue. For the objective about transportation systems, a guiding or essential question could be "Who controls today's transportation systems?" As is true of all questions of this type, it generates more questions, in this case about power relationships, who is rewarded and who pays, unintended consequences, and official policies, to name a few. For help in writing and using essential or guiding questions, see Wiggins and McTighe's *Understanding by Design* (2005) and Rob Traver's "What Is a Good Guiding Question?" (1998).

The terms for questions that guide instruction are used differently by different educators. Some educators use the term "essential question" to mean the topical question of the day's lesson. Do not let terminology distract you from developing several big questions that your lessons will address, at least in some partial way. When a student asks you, "Why do we have to know this?" respond in a way that clarifies practical applications of that learning, even if it's only, "Because it's how the real world works." When a student says, "I'm never gonna need to use this," the teacher who has thought about the ways that the curriculum connects with life outside of the classroom is in a much better position to treat the comment as a serious teachable moment.

Here, then, are elements commonly found in instructional plans:

- Identifying information (lesson topic, title, grade, dates)
- Associated academic standards, usually in the form of benchmarks
- Topical, essential, and guiding questions
- Instructional objectives
- Formative or summative assessment tasks
- Learning activities, which may include the following:
  — Introduction, hook, or anticipatory set. This may be in the form of a bellringer that students will begin to think about or work on as soon as they enter the classroom
  — Access to new information
  — Recording or saving new information for future reference

— Working with new content to make sense of it and connect it to prior knowledge

— Application or practice that may double as formative assessment, with varying degrees of teacher guidance and monitoring

• Differentiation plans for individual students who need it

• Closure that will prompt students to reflect on the content of the lesson and connect it to their own personal knowledge base and to other parts of the curriculum. The topical, guiding, or essential questions are often addressed in closure.

• Homework assignment

• Materials or preparation required

• Post-lesson reflection on how the lesson went and what could be changed for better results or for future students

Sample Plans for Student Learning

In Figure 10.1, you'll find a learning plan template that includes most of the elements we've just considered. The learning activities are organized into two columns: on the left, a description of what the students will do in class, and on the right, a description of what the teacher does to ensure that maximum learning is occurring while the students are engaged in those activities.

Figure 10.2 is a completed learning plan for middle school students, based on the template in Figure 10.1. Note that it is written in student-centered language, describing what students will do. Not only is this consistent with the focus on student learning that objectives and assessments require, but it also provides the creator of the plan as well as its readers with an understanding of what the students' experience of the lesson will be. We cannot think productively about students' thinking without imagining ourselves in their place, seeing school through their eyes.

Figure 10.1 • A Standard Learning Plan Format

Topic: **Title of Lesson:** **Standards:** **Essential Question(s):**

Objectives and Assessments (as many as needed, usually no more than three) Objective: Assessment: Formative [ ] Summative [ ] Objective: Assessment: Formative [ ] Summative [ ]

Learning Activities
Introduction:

How students will access new information (may include modeling):	How the teacher will monitor/check for understanding/give feedback:
How students will apply and/or process new information (review, organize, and work with it):	How the teacher will monitor/check for understanding/give feedback:

Independent practice (may be homework):

Closure:

Materials and Preparation
Materials that students will need:
Materials that the teacher will need:
Preparation for the lesson:

Differentiation Plans

Teacher Reflection (notes on strengths and difficulties; improvements for next time; ideas for follow-up)

Figure 10.2 • A Sample Learning Plan

Topic: Prepositional phrases

Title of Lesson: Introduction: Prepositions Are Everywhere!

Standards: Students manipulate the parts of speech effectively and employ a variety of sentence structures to communicate.

a. Use forms of nouns, pronouns, verbs, adjectives and their modifiers, adverbs, prepositions, transitions, conjunctions, and interjections correctly.*

Essential Question(s):

— How do we add information to basic sentences?

— Who decides what's right or wrong about the way we speak and write?

— How do children learn about their language?

Objectives and Assessments

Objective 1: Students will identify prepositional phrases, prepositions, and the objects of prepositions in texts they read and write.

Assessment 1: At first silently and independently, and then orally for the whole class, students will identify prepositional phrases, prepositions, and the objects of prepositions in the novel the class is reading. Later, they will write a two-paragraph piece (fiction or nonfiction) using at least five different prepositions and underline the prepositional phrases.

Formative [X] Summative [ ]

Objective 2: Students will explain the function of prepositional phrases.

Assessment 2a: In a discussion, students will explain the function of prepositions, based on their reading and writing.

Formative [X] Summative [ ]

Assessment 2b: To test and expand their understanding, students will read a paragraph projected on the board and then each will rewrite the paragraph, omitting prepositional phrases. This will be followed by a short journal entry explaining the contributions that prepositional phrases make to this paragraph and to our language overall.

Formative [X] Summative [ ]

Learning Activities

Introduction: Students will examine a picture of a snake near a fence. They will identify the ways that the snake can get to the other side of the fence: go under the fence, around the fence, over the fence, through the fence, etc. A student will write these phrases on the board as they are said. If no student can name this kind of phrase, I will provide it. The student scribe will write it on the board: "prepositional phrase."

* This learning plan is based on standard D1a from Maine's English Language Arts standards, grades 6–8 (Maine Department of Education, 2007, p. 20).

continued

Figure 10.2 • A Sample Learning Plan (*continued*)

How students will access new information (a continuation of the lesson introduction):	How the teacher will monitor/check for understanding/give feedback:
Students will identify the words in each phrase written on the board that are different from the words the phrases have in common ("the fence"): *through, around, under, over.* If students don't know what part of speech these words are, several students will each use a dictionary to look up one of the words and report the part of speech. The student recorder writes "preposition" on the board. If no student can name the role that "fence" plays, I will provide it, and the scribe will write it on the board: "object of the preposition." Students generate a few examples of prepositional phrases, noting prepositions and objects.	The art of guiding students through this discovery process lies in seeing what they can figure out and look up on their own, and when they genuinely need help. Time is also a factor: we can't afford to spend too much time on finding names for parts of speech, since the real learning of them will come with later activities. I prefer to have students look up words we need information about, but I may skip that step if time is slipping away too quickly.
How students will apply and/or process new information (review, organize, and work with it):	**How the teacher will monitor/check for understanding/give feedback:**
1. A student will draw two classmates' names from a hat. The first student drawn will be the reporter; the second will be the actor. From a collection of props, the actor will select objects and perform actions that the reporter will describe, using prepositional phrases. For example, the actor may tie a sash *around his waist* or put a rubber frog *in his pocket* and a plastic apple *on his head.* He may also adopt positions (such as hands on hips) that do not use the props, and it is the reporter's job to describe the actions, using prepositional phrases (a lifted foot is *in the air,* for example). The reporter will speak these phrases as the actions are performed and write the phrases on the board. The goal is to see that we use prepositional phrases to provide information and to generate a list of these phrases. Once the roles have been repeated several times with different students, everyone will examine the list of phrases on the board and generate more from their imaginations. The teacher may contribute some as well.	I will explain the activity and demonstrate one possible way to use the props and to describe their use with prepositional phrases. Then I will ask for another "action suggestion" from the students and ask the student who offers one to perform it. If some students still have questions, I will tell them to hold them until they have seen the action performed several times. During this activity, I will monitor continuously and provide guidance in the form of questions if students need it. I hope this activity will generate positive feelings toward prepositions that will color attitudes toward the following activities. I must look for signs of comprehension or confusion in all students at this early stage and interject questions to those who look unsure.

2. Students will turn to the selected passage in the text they have been reading and locate the prepositional phrases—first independently and silently, and then aloud as they are randomly selected to report out. In each case, the student will identify the preposition and the object of the preposition and will also note whether other words are in the phrase. A student will write these prepositions on the board as they are mentioned.	This activity will be easy for some students and difficult for others. I will instruct those who are having trouble to look for selected prepositions (*on, for, with*) to identify those phrases and ignore others. I will add more prepositions to the student's list of what to look for, as appropriate.
3. Students will read a paragraph projected on the board. Then each student will rewrite the paragraph, omitting prepositional phrases. In pairs, students will read the results to each other, making sure that all prepositional phrases have been omitted. Then, in a short class discussion, students will explain the purposes of prepositional phrases, after which they will follow up with a journal entry about the uses of prepositional phrases, including examples.	The purpose of this activity is for students to discover how brief and empty many sentences become when prepositional phrases are removed. Some may be uncomfortable with this because they won't recognize the remaining sentence as a sentence if it is reduced to something like "My house is." This is an opportunity to remind them of earlier lessons on sentences and prompt them reread their notebook entry on what makes a sentence complete.
Independent practice: Students will write two paragraphs on a topic of their choice, using at least six prepositional phrases. The goal is to practice using prepositional phrases as part of communicating.	**How the teacher will monitor/check for understanding/give feedback:** As students write, I will circulate, interrupting the writing process only when a correction is essential (that is, when a student is not yet ready for truly independent practice).

Closure: Consulting their language notebooks, students will briefly review the parts of speech they have learned so far: nouns, pronouns, verbs, adjectives, and adverbs. They will discuss two questions: (1) "Can a phrase serve as one or more of these parts of speech?" and (2) "Which parts of speech can a prepositional phrase be?" Then they will add "phrase" and "prepositional phrase," with examples of each, to their notebooks. Finally, they will discuss the value of knowing how to recognize and use these parts of speech.

continued

Figure 10.2 • A Sample Learning Plan (*continued*)

Materials and Preparation

Materials that students will need

- Paper and pencil/pen
- A copy of text we are reading or have recently read

Materials that the teacher will need:

- Picture of snake and fence
- Items that can be used by "actors"
- Student names on slips of paper for drawing
- List of prepositional phrases to contribute to students' brainstorming session, including some prepositions that do not directly describe location: *about, after, until, without, except.*
- Paragraph to display to class for assessment #2
- Selected passage from the text the class is reading or has recently read that contains prepositional phrases.

Preparation for the lesson: I plan to project a picture of a snake and fence through the computer, but if that doesn't work, I will just sketch a fence and snake on the board—or ask Donny to do so (he's a much better artist than I am). But I will practice beforehand and use my small sketch as a guide for a larger version on the board or as a guide for Donny so that he can see what I have in mind.

Differentiation Plan

- If Sarah becomes confused or frustrated by the number of prepositions that come up in this lesson, I will tell her to focus on three common ones: *on, for,* and *with.* For the moment, she can ignore the others.
- I'll need to try to keep Jason from getting overexcited by the "acting." As soon as he enters the classroom, I will tell him privately that we are going to play a short game today and that his job is to concentrate on learning from it, as I will be calling on him afterward.
- Because April writes very slowly, I will be near her desk so that I can tell her privately that she can use some abbreviations and show her the shortcuts she can take. I will pair her up with Caitlin.

Teacher Reflection

- This lesson is a kind of discovery lesson, so there was very little direct instruction, and the only modeling was a brief demonstration of what to do with the props. However, I need to remember that when discovery isn't working, I have to be ready to insert some selected direct instruction for individual students who don't have the interest or patience to figure things out. I did have to watch the students carefully to make sure nobody was getting frustrated or confused by the number of possible forms that prepositional phrases can take—Sarah isn't the only one who likes learning to come in neat, manageable packages, and I did have to tell her and Jon to concentrate on the three common prepositions at the beginning. After they worked with partners, they got the hang of it.

- Donny is intellectually as well as artistically gifted, and he zoomed through the final writing. He knows that he can always create drawings to accompany his writing, and this time he produced some very creative illustrations of "hit the snowman with fine spray from our water pistols" to create a "glassy-skinned monster with a permanent drip on its nose."
- This group did well with the lesson, but I can see that if there were more students who had trouble staying mentally flexible, I would need to slow it down and focus everyone on a just a few common prepositions until they were comfortable with the pattern. As it was, I emphasized that they were learning a pattern of a phrase, not memorizing individual prepositions or prepositional phrases.
- Next in the study of prepositional phrases are the modifiers that can be inserted between the preposition and its object. Further ahead, we'll learn about prepositional phrases that use pronouns instead of nouns—that will be a challenge, especially with *me, her, and him!*

There are many formats that do not clearly spotlight the main elements listed on pages 180–181, although they are likely to include other elements. The sample lesson in Figure 10.3 shows one of these variations. Here, the objectives are not identified as such but are embedded in the benchmark and in the description of content. Assessment follows the description of instructional methods or procedures rather than being positioned up front next to the outcomes with which it is aligned. As you read this plan, consider what is gained or lost in this way of displaying the conceptual work the teacher has done to prepare for students' learning.

As you encounter various formats for learning plans, look for what's missing as well as what's present. Consider the context, the audience, and the purpose of using a particular format. You'll find that some are set up to help the teacher work out ideas and create a detailed map of the path to learning (which is what this book addresses), some are designed for easy sharing with colleagues, some allow easy review by administrators who want to ensure a lesson addresses standards and assessments, and some are pitched as ideal for a teaching portfolio.

Beginners need to include more information in learning plans than experienced professionals do. A format that requires details helps beginners remember that generalities are a mark of unfinished planning. Experienced professionals know that specific descriptions of student thinking and

Figure 10.3 • Sample Learning Plan Format with Objectives Embedded

Title: Changing Life-Forms
Primary Subject: Biology
Secondary Subjects: Art and writing
Grade Level: 4
Content: Students will compare living and extinct plants and animals. They will discuss, write about, and draw changes in living things over time.
Benchmarks: Recognize that fossils provide us with information about living things that inhabited the Earth long ago.*

Learning Resources and Materials:
1. Clip from *Walking with Dinosaurs*
2. Assignment handout for booklet or poster
3. Webquest sites
4. Worksheet on which students record information
5. Paper and pencils for drawing

Development of Lesson:

	What Teacher Will Do	What Students Will Do
Introduction	Show a clip of *Walking with Dinosaurs* and guide students in a discussion of characteristics of dinosaurs and their habitats and possible reasons they died out.	Watch the video clip and discuss characteristics of dinosaurs and their habitats and possible reasons they died out.
Methods/Procedures	1. Tell students what they will be learning and that, after several days of study, they will create a booklet or poster that shows some changes in life-forms over time. Hand out assignment description of the booklet or poster so students can begin to think about which they will choose.	1. Listen to information about upcoming work, read handout, and consider their choice of booklet or poster.
	2. Guide students in a webquest that takes them to sites providing information about fossils of extinct animals and the plants in their habitats. Provide a worksheet on which students record information they will need.	2. Conduct a webquest to gather information about fossils of extinct animals and the plants in their habitats. Record information on worksheet.

* This learning plan is based on the Pennsylvania academic standard 3.1.3.C3: Evolution: Constancy and Change (Commonwealth of Pennsylvania Department of Education, 2011).

	What Teacher Will Do	What Students Will Do
Assessment/Evaluation	1. Conduct informal formative assessment based on observations of learning that occurs during the webquest and note taking on the worksheet. In addition to reading worksheet notes, I will frequently ask students to tell me what they are seeing, reading, and learning from the webquest. When I see that someone is not understanding what a website presents, I will point out what the student should be paying attention to, and explain in simpler terms if necessary. Then I will require the student to make notes and re-explain to me so that I know he or she won't forget these points.	1. Show and tell what they are writing and learning in response to teacher questions. Ask questions as needed.
	2. Assess formatively during closure, when students brainstorm a statement about how we know about extinct life-forms and draw an illustration for it. The statement that the class generates will probably not show me what every student understands, but their individual drawings will, so as I circulate, I will remind them to focus on aligning their drawings with the statement. When I am satisfied that each one understands the content of this lesson, I may ask some students to label elements of their drawings, or to add a caption that explains their thinking, just so that they remember this information.	2. Engage in brainstorming to generate a statement about extinct life-forms and draw an illustration for it.
Closure	1. Bring the students into a discussion circle to talk about memorable facts and pictures on the websites and about the understanding they are developing about changes that have occurred in animals and plants revealed in the fossil record.	1. Discuss their experiences with the webquest, including what was most memorable. They will ask and answer questions about the changes that have occurred and about how we know what we know. They will respond to one other's ideas.
	2. Guide the students in creating a summarizing statement that they all agree on (if individuals want to express the idea in their own words, they may) and in sketching an illustration of this statement. They can use the sketch later in their booklet or poster, if they wish.	2. After discussion, brainstorm a summarizing statement that they and I agree on, and sketch an illustration of this statement. They will use the sketch later in their booklet or poster, if they wish.

continued

Figure 10.3 • Sample Learning Plan Format with Objectives Embedded (*continued*)

Teacher Reflection:

This topic has the potential to be great because most kids like dinosaurs, and the idea that plants and animals are dying out, coming into being, and changing right now is pretty fascinating, as is the idea that we have a fossil record and are leaving our own evidence for future generations to discover. However, I could see that two of the websites I chose for the webquest were a little too sophisticated for about half the students. Next time, I will put the students in pairs and encourage them to study sites together when they want to—some social kids will want to talk their way through the whole process, whereas others will want to think their own thoughts and go at their own paces. I'll have to work that out for individuals.

Otherwise, the webquest accomplished what I wanted it to. As always, students vary enormously in the kinds of notes they take, so I keep reminding them to focus on the point of the question and make sure they answered that. Then, if they want to write down more information, they are welcome to. Several students wanted to show a family member at home interesting stuff they were finding, so I suggested that they could just use separate sheets of paper to record the URLs or site titles they could search for. I love it when they take learning home!

The closure discussion was a little tricky because I wanted it to be informal and as spontaneous as possible, but I wanted to be sure that I heard from Jerry, Chris, and Tracy, who disengage unless I'm on them. I had decided that I would call on each of them early on (but not in succession) and if their answers were sketchy, tell them I would return to them, which I did. After the discussion, Chris and Tracy, who like to draw, thought about what they were going to illustrate, but Jerry resisted. Finally, I asked him to imagine that he had to send a letter to a friend his age who couldn't read—but the friend needed to understand the sentence the class had brainstormed in order to win a prize. The only way Jerry could help his friend would be to sketch the idea, even if it was just stick figures. It was kind of a wild shot, but Jerry is protective of his friends and sympathetic with not knowing school stuff (like reading), so it more or less worked. Some other students produced beautiful drawings. I think I will post the drawings of everyone who volunteers them for the duration of this lesson. I want students to be reminded that they will be using drawing in the booklet or poster, and this gets them started in thinking about how to illustrate ideas. Drawing also consolidates information and makes it the student's own.

performing are necessary. Keep in mind, too, that a learning plan format could be missing something important because the person who created it didn't understand how to think about students' learning.

The final sample learning plan, in Figure 10.4, uses terminology common to some formats that can obscure the basic elements all learning plans should have (see pp. 180–181). As you review this plan, try to identify these elements and then rephrase the ideas to clarify what the student learning outcomes are intended to be and how they will be taught and assessed. See if you can also explain what the other elements (perhaps some of Hunter's?) would contribute to student learning in this plan. What else do you notice about this plan, either about the template or about the way the lesson is described?

These three formats for recording a plan for student learning just begin to illustrate the range of ways you might lay out your own ideas. These different formats also underscore the complexities inherent in the planning process. There are many variables and choices, and many responsibilities to be fulfilled—responsibilities you have to students, who follow your lead, and also responsibilities you have to follow the district curriculum and the state or national academic standards and responsibilities to address the skills and knowledge (such as reading, writing, and collaborating) that should be practiced frequently regardless of the primary focus of the lesson.

Figure 10.4 • Sample Lesson Plan Format with Multiple Additional Elements

Subject: Math

Grade: 3

Ability Level: Mixed

Teacher's Objective: To improve students' understanding of word problems by having them create and solve their own. To give students practice in solving word problems, and to evaluate their abilities.

Standards/Benchmarks: PO 2—Create and solve word problems based on addition, subtraction, multiplication, and division.*

Overview/Narrative: Most students find word problems to be difficult because they have to figure out what they need to figure out, so creating their own problems should help them with this process.

Purpose: To give students insight into the connections between word problems, numerical operations, and math problems that occur in everyday life.

Description: I will model the process of creating a word problem from an everyday situation and then solve that problem. Then students will create another word problem, with my guidance, and solve it. In pairs, students will create their own word problem, which they will solve themselves, then exchange with another pair.

Vocabulary: word problem, relevant information, unnecessary information, numerical operation

Interdisciplinary Connections: Language arts and math

Extension Ideas: Students can write a story that involves solving a math problem.

* This learning plan is based on the Arizona mathematics standard for grade 3, Strand 1: Number and Operation, Concept 2: Numerical Operations (Arizona Department of Education, 2008, p. 2.).

continued

Figure 10.4 • Sample Lesson Plan Format with Multiple Additional Elements
(*continued*)

Performance Expectations: Students will create and solve word problems involving addition, subtraction, multiplication, and division.

Primary Teaching Methods Used: Direct instruction and cooperative learning

Sequence of Learning Activities:

1. *Anticipatory set:* Tell students I have a problem that I need their help with: My son plays in Little League and gets home from practice at about 6:15 p.m. He has to do homework before he can watch his favorite TV show at 8:00 p.m., and his bedtime is 9:00 p.m., right after the show. If he needs to set aside an hour for homework, and dinner generally takes about half an hour, what time should I have dinner on the table?

As I tell this little story, I will write notes on the board so students can see the times involved, beginning with 6:15 and a sketch of a baseball bat. I'll put dinner and homework down but without clock times— only the amount of time they require. I can sketch a TV next to a clock face showing 8:00 p.m. Then I'll ask students what we need to figure out in order to answer the question about dinnertime.

Some students will see that they need to work backward from 8:00 p.m., subtracting an hour so that homework begins no later than 7:00. Working backward again, they will be able to see that dinner should be no later than 6:30.

Then we can tell the whole chronology of my son's evening. I'll ask what kind of problem they just solved. If they don't say that they needed to use subtraction, I'll focus their attention on the operation they used. Eventually we should get to the terms of operation, which I'll write on the board for their reference.

2. *Development of the lesson:* I'll tell students that they'll be writing their own word problems in a few minutes, but first we'll create one together. I'll ask them to think about something they use math for outside of school—something they count or figure out that uses the four basic operations they know. "Counting" may bring up money or something they collect, and "figuring things out" might bring up any kind of problem, having to do with math or not. Money, time, and quantities of other items seem most likely. I'll guide them through a process of using real-life situations as well as imagination and make-believe to invent a word problem. We'll begin small, with something like "If my father and my grandmother each give me five dollars for my birthday, how much money will I have?" To make the problem more complicated, we will add more of the story, such as how much will be left after I've bought a toy that costs seven dollars.

3. After we've solved our collective problem by working through the steps, I'll give students some time to brainstorm some individual problems, using sentence starters like "How much time [money] . . .?" and "If I want . . .?" and "If I have . . . and my friend has . . . ." After everyone has had time to think about a "story" that requires mathematical operations, I'll tell students that they can work alone or with a partner to write out their word problems. If they work with a partner, each person has to come up with a separate problem, but they can help each other do that. They don't have to solve the problems yet, just write them. I'll circulate as students work. When someone finishes, I might ask this person to help someone who's having trouble. I will also tell those who have the kind of problem I'm looking for—not too simple, but solvable—to write it on the board.

4. While students work, I'll privately ask different students to solve one of the problems on the board and be ready to explain it to the class. If any student has trouble, I'll provide a personalized walk-through of the steps or ask another student who's finished to help.

5. When we finish solving and reviewing the problems on the board, I'll ask if anyone else wants to read their problem to the class. I'll also ask whether anyone has a problem they can't solve. If they do, we'll go through it together as a class, working out what information we have, what information we're trying to figure out, and what information we need to have to do this.

Closure (reflects anticipatory set):
After we have worked on creating and solving word problems, I'll ask students what they remember about the problem with my son's schedule. What was the situation? What information did we have? What did we have to figure out? How did we solve it?

Evaluation:
Students will be evaluated on their work using this three-point scale:

3 points: Students demonstrated proficiency in creating and solving word problems; worked cooperatively with other students to write and solve word problems; contributed to class discussions about creating and solving word problems.

2 points: Students demonstrated an understanding of how to create and solve word problems; worked somewhat cooperatively with other students to write and solve word problems; contributed somewhat to class discussions about creating and solving word problems.

1 point: Students had difficulty in creating and solving word problems; resisted working cooperatively with other students to write and solve word problems; contributed minimally or not at all to class discussions about creating and solving word problems.

Reinforcement: For homework, students will take home a word problem template that requires them to fill in some blanks but that also sets the story up so they can't get too lost or confused (it's a little like that game where you fill in adjectives, nouns, etc.). I'll explain that the choices they will make are just the quantities, and if they find that they can't solve the problem with the quantities they put in (too large or too small), they can go back and change them. The template will take them step-by-step through the process of figuring out what they know and what they need to know and what operation they need to perform.

Comments: Word problems weren't new to these students, but this was the first time they had to create their own. As always, some students got it right away and some stayed confused for a while. However, I kept the confused ones working on a very simple level of counting this and counting that and then adding them together. The fast workers I encouraged to make the problems more complicated and interesting—but still solvable. I wish there had been five of me to circulate and keep track of everyone, but once we came together to work on the problems that students had written on the board, and selected students explained how to solve them, I asked some of the previously confused students to restate the solution after the first student had explained it. I do this a lot—asking students to answer a question someone else has just answered so that they keep listening and thinking, so this was a familiar experience.

PRACTICE EXERCISE: Creating a Plan for Student Learning

Revisit the objective, assessment, rubric, and learning activities that you have created and assemble them into a learning plan, following the format in Figures 10.1 and 10.2. As you think about your students learning from the activities, decide what you, as the teacher, will need to focus on while they do this work. In a general sense, you will be monitoring students' progress toward mastering the objective, but if you pin down the specifics of what you will be looking for, listening for, and thinking about, as well as how you might respond to students' questions or difficulties, you will be that much better prepared to teach this lesson.

As you go through this process, pay attention to how you are using your objectives for every step. A novice who does not yet fully understand objectives or assessments may be tempted to cross them off the list of things to do once they are written and then stop thinking about them, but objectives and assessments must be front and center when making decisions about the rest of the learning plan. Effective teachers use their objectives continuously when they are designing instruction and when they are teaching.

Working through the process of creating a plan for learning reveals what good preparation for teaching really entails. If you find you are resistant to answering all the questions implicit in a given format, remember that—provided the format is well designed—these are questions that you must answer sooner or later, and if you do not answer them as best you can before teaching the lesson, you may well have to answer them in the middle of the lesson, when you are not expecting them and have no time to reflect.

Another thing a teacher can learn from working through the process of creating a learning plan is why teaching from someone else's plan is often difficult, uncomfortable, and not fully successful. This is especially the case when you're using only a learning activity rather than a full plan. Directing a learning activity without thinking through its relation to its objectives leaves a teacher uncertain of what to look for during the lesson and, thus, not fully prepared to guide students to a desired end point.

Each plan for learning that you design will make it that much easier to design future ones, so do not become discouraged if the early plans take a great deal of time and effort.

Additional Resources for Creating Learning Plans

A teacher's biggest challenge in using the many, many resources on lesson design that are currently available is sorting through them to identify those that provide the fullest possible support for student learning. Here are some that my students have found helpful:

***Classroom Instruction That Works,* by Robert J. Marzano, Deborah J. Pickering, and Jane E. Pollock (2001)**

The basis of this book is the examination of nine methods of generating, directing, and supporting students' thinking, such as identifying similarities and differences, summarizing and note taking, and homework and practice. Research supports the effectiveness of the strategies covered, which should be in every teacher's instructional repertoire. These strategies can be adapted to almost any grade and subject, and the authors provide numerous examples of practical applications.

***Checking for Understanding: Formative Assessment Techniques for Your Classroom,* by Douglas Fisher and Nancy Frey (2007)**

Finding out what students understand is part of the instructional process, and its importance cannot be overstated. Although it is the only way to know when the purpose of teaching—student learning—has been accomplished, it is often passed over lightly in many classrooms. The authors of this book discuss in detail a wide range of ways to check for understanding, from hand signals during a lesson to formal tests closing a unit or program.

Their techniques can be adapted for all subjects and all grades, and they fit smoothly into routines of instruction and assessment.

How to Assess Higher-Order Thinking Skills in Your Classroom, by Susan M. Brookhart (2010)

This is a clear, practical guide to exactly what the title says: assessing higher-order thinking skills. By laying out many examples of ways to assess logic and reasoning, analysis, evaluation, judgment, problem solving, and creativity, the author shows readers that they can successfully teach and assess higher-order thinking. Teachers can extend the use of these ideas into establishing instructional objectives and designing learning activities that can be adapted to virtually all subjects at all grade levels.

The Multiple Intelligences of Reading and Writing: Making the Words Come Alive, by Thomas Armstrong (2003)

Most of us are not fully aware of how differently reading and writing are experienced by different people. The author of this book explores these differences to show how thinking of text solely as marks on a page is an unnecessarily limiting approach that won't help learners who benefit from connecting literacy with other natural behavior—kinesthetic, artistic, musical, logical, and so on. This book opens up many possibilities not only for teaching but also for thinking about your students' ways of interacting with text and, more generally, about their ways of learning.

Differentiated Instruction in the English Classroom: Content, Process, Product, and Assessment, by Barbara King-Shaver and Alyce Hunter (2003)

The intended audience for this book is middle and high school English teachers, but it will expand horizons for teachers of other subjects as well. The authors explain the purposes of differentiating instruction; they grapple with potentially difficult subjects such as grading and management in a heterogeneous classroom (and point out that virtually all classrooms are heterogeneous, even when they are tracked). Many specific examples and case studies illustrate how to take steps toward meeting different students' needs without undue stress on either teacher or student.

Brain Matters: Translating Research into Classroom Practice, **(2nd edition), by Patricia Wolfe (2010)**

In an ideal world, all teachers would know as much about the human brain and learning as this book provides. The first third is a thorough but reader-friendly explanation of brain structures and their functions. The examples of classroom practice that follow are not new, but they are explained in terms of their compatibility with brain function, which may also be thought of as "natural ways of learning." Although the author does not directly address the ways in which this knowledge can help a teacher understand what is or isn't working for particular students, that potential is there. This book is best read as background for understanding learning, considered in conjunction with practical instructional and assessment techniques.

Afterword

We began this study of designing instruction by noting that most students have, at best, a partial view of the work that teachers do because so much of this work occurs when they are not present to witness it.

Novice teachers entering the profession tend to have a similarly incomplete view. As teachers gain experience, they learn to see behind the scenes and come to understand that the classroom performance of effective teaching is reliant on extensive preparation, which itself is based on extensive thinking. But until this shift is made, a teacher's focus will still be on outward behavior, meaning that the success of a lesson is likely to be measured in terms of students' levels of engagement with classroom activities and their cooperation with classroom rules. The assumption that "if students are busy, they must be thinking and learning" keeps the students' intellectual work as hidden from the teacher as the teacher's intellectual work is from the students.

In this book, we've looked at how to make the shift—how to see beyond the performance of "ritualized routines" (Nuthall, 2005) of lectures, worksheets, reading and homework assignments, and various other classroom activities and get to the point when you know in your bones that your intellectual work—the imagining, analyzing, synthesizing, preparing, and creating you do when there are no students around—is the first and most important step toward effective instruction.

The benefits of this "deep design" planning for students' learning rather than for directing classroom activity are obvious when the lesson and learning go well, but the benefits are even more obvious when the lesson does not proceed smoothly. A teacher who understands how to design instruction for student learning is in a much better position to see what is going wrong and figure how to remedy the problem. When, for example, students resist doing the learning activities called for in a lesson, or do not do them in the manner intended, a teacher who is clear about objectives and is guiding the students' thinking can see where the students are in relation to the new content and make midcourse corrections on the spot.

Successful teachers know how to think about their students' thinking. They attend carefully to what students know and do not know, plan what students will learn and how they will learn it, and then check to see whether the learning occurred. The challenge, then, is to understand what intellectual work requires of students and what teachers do to bring it about. Thinking in a disciplined and creative way about students' thinking is where our teaching and their learning begin. It's how we get the real work done.

Appendix A

The Revised Bloom's Taxonomy

Each of the six categories in the revised Bloom's taxonomy developed by Anderson and colleagues (2001) is a mental skill or ability that individuals may learn to use. We can demonstrate mastery of these skills and abilities by engaging in certain activities. In general, the list proceeds from simpler skills to more complex ones, and to some extent, the simpler abilities (such as remembering) are necessary for mastery of more complex abilities (such as applying). In many cases, practicing more complex skills promotes mastery of simpler ones, as when analysis results in firmer comprehension of an idea.

1. **Remember**—*to pull past knowledge into present consciousness.*
This is the simplest mental skill. We use our memories when we *recognize* something we've encountered before. Answering "Which of these numbers is one thousand?" or "Which of these animals is a mammal?" requires that someone recognize the correct answer in an assortment of possibilities. *Recall* can be more challenging to memory, since we must generate the correct answer rather than simply recognize it. Remembering the answer to "What is this number?" or "What are the characteristics of mammals?" requires recollection when a choice of answers is not provided.

2. **Comprehend/Understand**—*to grasp the meaning of something.*
We can remember or recognize information without understanding it, as when we have memorized the definition of a word but don't really know what it means. When we do understand, we can express information or concepts in our own words or explain what meaning we are making of a new situation or idea. We can also summarize the new information and explain how it is like or different from something else we understand.

3. **Apply**—*to use knowledge and/or skills to bring about a desired result.*
Applying knowledge requires both that we know (can remember) it and that we understand it. Applying new knowledge is also one of the best kinds of practice to ensure that we can remember and understand that knowledge in the future.

4. **Analyze**—*to break the whole into its parts.*
Analysis allows us to learn more of the nature of something by distinguishing its components and figuring out how those components relate to one another and to the purpose or nature of the whole.

5. **Evaluate**—*to determine the value or worth of something according to specified criteria.*
To evaluate, we must have knowledge of what is being judged as well as knowledge of the judgment criteria.

6. **Create/Synthesize**—*to create is to bring something new into being; to synthesize is to bring elements together into new formations.*
The new forms referred to here are likely to be something that is new to us rather than new to human history. The elements we use for creation and synthesis may come from widely disparate sources.

Learning More

A search of the Internet and other media will provide a huge number of sources for information about Bloom's taxonomy and its revision by Anderson and colleagues. However, these sources must be used judiciously, as all charts, wheels, pyramids, and other displays of Bloom's ideas will include examples of types of thinking and related skills that some educators will find misleading if not downright wrong. Even when an example could be agreed upon as legitimate for one particular situation, it might be inappropriate for another. That is why it is essential to test each verb and noun for its accuracy as a description of student learning or assessment and to avoid taking the shortcut of assuming that if it's on a list, it must be right.

The two websites below provide helpful graphic displays of information, but here, too, the user must test each suggested verb for suitability in statements of learning outcomes:

- From Richard C. Overbaugh and Lynn Schultz, **www.odu.edu/educ/roverbau/Bloom/blooms_taxonomy.htm** provides a nice illustration of the similarities and differences between the original taxonomy and the revision by Anderson and colleagues. The pyramid format is a graphic display of the idea that the higher levels of intellectual skills rest on a foundation of lower levels and that a broad base of factual knowledge is essential to developing higher levels of skills and knowledge.

- From Iowa State University, **www.celt.iastate.edu/teaching/Revised Blooms1.html** includes a mouse-over graphic that provides examples of skills associated with each level of the taxonomy. It also summarizes additional information from the 2001 revision.

Appendix B

National Standards from Professional Organizations

Subject Area	Description	URL
Art	Standards for art education for all grade levels produced by the National Association for Music Education (NAfME) for the Consortium of National Arts Education Associations	http://artsedge.kennedy-center.org/educators/standards.aspx
English/ Language Arts	Twelve general standards for language arts produced by the National Council of Teachers of English (NCTE) and the International Reading Association (IRA); a full explanation and examples of lessons are available in a downloadable book format	http://www.ncte.org/standards
Foreign Languages	Standards for foreign language education from the American Council on the Teaching of Foreign Languages (ACTFL)	http://www.actfl.org
Geography	Eighteen standards for geography produced by the National Council for Geographic Education (NCGE)	http://www.ncge.org
History	Standards for history for all grades produced by the National Center for History in the Schools (NCHS)	http://www.sscnet.ucla.edu/nchs/standards
Mathematics	Standards for mathematics for all grades produced by the National Council of Teachers of Mathematics (NCTM); lesson examples are included	http://standards.nctm.org

Subject Area	Description	URL
Music	Nine standards for music education produced by the National Association for Music Education (NAfME)	http://www.menc.org/resources/view/performance-standards-for-music-standards-publications
Physical Education	Standards for physical education from the National Association for Sport and Physical Education (NASPE); a full explanation of the standards is available only in a book available for purchase	http://www.aahperd.org/whatwedo/nationalstandards.cfm
Science	Standards for science for all grades produced by the National Research Council; example lessons and assessments are included	http://www.nap.edu/openbook.php?record_id=4962
Social Studies	Standards for social studies for all grades produced by the National Council for the Social Studies (NCSS); a full list of standards by grade level, including lesson examples, is available only in a book, but a description of the 10 strands—the themes by which the standards are organized—is available online	http://www.socialstudies.org/standards

References

Anderson, L. W., Krathwohl, D. R., Airasian, P., Cruikshank, K., Mayer, R., Pintrich, P., . . . & Wittrock, M. (Eds.). (2001). *A taxonomy for learning, teaching, and assessing: A revision of Bloom's taxonomy of educational objectives*. New York: Longman.

Arizona Department of Education—Standards and Assessment Division (2008, August). *Mathematics standards articulated by grade level—Strand 1: Number and operations*. Retrieved May 5, 2011, from http://www.ade.az.gov/standards/math/Articulated08/MathGradesK-6bystrand.pdf

Armstrong, T. (2003). *The multiple intelligences of reading and writing: Making the words come alive*. Alexandria, VA: ASCD.

Biology Online. (n.d.). Thinking. Retrieved from http://www.biology-online.org/dictionary/thinking

Bloom, B. S. (Ed.). (1956). *Taxonomy of educational objectives: The classification of educational goals. Handbook I: Cognitive domain*. New York: David McKay.

Brookhart, S. M. (2010). *How to assess higher-order thinking skills in your classroom*. Alexandria, VA: ASCD.

Common Core State Standards Initiative. (2010a). *Common core state standards for English language arts & literacy in history/social studies, science, and technical subjects*. Retrieved from http://www.corestandards.org/assets/CCSSI_ELA%20Standards.pdf

Common Core State Standards Initiative. (2010b). *Common core state standards for mathematics—Grade 3—Number & operations—Fractions*. Retrieved from http://www.corestandards.org/the-standards/mathematics/grade-3/number-and-operations-fractions

Common Core State Standards Initiative. (2010c). *Common core state standards for mathematics—Grade 6—Statistics & probability.* Retrieved from http://www.corestandards.org/the-standards/mathematics/grade-6/statistics-and-probability

Common Core State Standards Initiative. (2010d). *Common core state standards for mathematics—High school: Number & quantity—The complex number system.* Retrieved from http://www.corestandards.org/the-standards/mathematics/hs-number-and-quantity/the-complex-number-system

Commonwealth of Pennsylvania Department of Education. (2011). *Academic standards.* Retrieved from http://www.pdesas.org/Standard

Danielson, C. (2007). *Enhancing professional practice: A framework for teaching* (2nd ed.). Alexandria, VA: ASCD.

Fisher, D., & Frey, N. (2007). *Checking for understanding: Formative assessment techniques for your classroom.* Alexandria, VA: ASCD.

Goleman, D. (1995). *Emotional intelligence: Why it can matter more than IQ.* New York: Bantam.

Hunter, M. (1982). *Mastery teaching.* El Segundo, CA: TIP publications.

Hunter, M., & Russell, D. (1994). Planning for effective instruction: Lesson design. In M. Hunter (Ed.), *Enhancing teaching* (pp. 87–95). New York: Macmillan College Publishing.

King-Shaver, B., & Hunter, A. (2003). *Differentiated instruction in the English classroom: Content, process, product, and assessment.* Portsmouth, NH: Heinemann.

Krathwohl, D. R., Bloom, B. S., & Masia, B. B. (1964). *Taxonomy of educational objectives: The classification of education goals. Handbook II: Affective domain.* New York: David McKay.

Mager, R. (1984). *Goal analysis* (2nd ed.). Belmont, CA: David S. Lake Publishers.

Maine Department of Education (2007). *Regulation 131. Learning results: Parameters for essential instruction.* Retrieved from http://www.maine.gov/education/lres/pei/ela102207.pdf

Marzano, R. J., Pickering, D. J., & Pollock, J. E. (2001). *Classroom instruction that works: Research-based strategies for increasing student achievement.* Alexandria, VA: ASCD.

McTighe, J., & Ferrara, S. (2000). *Assessing learning in the classroom.* Washington, DC: National Education Association.

Noddings, N. (1984). *Caring: A feminine approach to ethics and moral education.* Berkeley: University of California Press.

Nuthall, G. (2005). The cultural myths and realities of classroom teaching and learning: A personal journey. *Teachers College Record, 107*(5), 895–934.

Oregon Department of Education. (2001, April). *Academic standards for social sciences.* Retrieved from http://www.ode.state.or.us/teachlearn/real/documents/ss.pdf

Reeves, A. (2004). *Adolescents talk about reading: Exploring resistance to and engagement with text.* Newark, DE: International Reading Association.

Texas Department of Education. (2010, August). *Chapter 113. Texas essential knowledge and skills for social students—Subchapter B—Middle school. knowledge and skills for social studies.* Retrieved from http://ritter.tea.state.tx.us/rules/tac/chapter113/ch113b.html

Traver, R. (1998, March). What is a good guiding question? *Educational Leadership, 55*(6), 70–73.

Wiggins, G., & McTighe, J. (2005). *Understanding by design.* Alexandria, VA: ASCD.

Wolfe, P. (2010). *Brain matters: Translating research into classroom practice* (2nd ed.). Alexandria, VA: ASCD.

Index

The letter *f* following a page number denotes a figure.

About the Author

Anne R. Reeves is an associate professor of education and department head at Susquehanna University, a small, private, liberal-arts undergraduate college in Selinsgrove, Pennsylvania. She teaches introductory education courses to first-year students, teaches methods courses to seniors, and supervises secondary education students in their student teaching.

Dr. Reeves is a member of the board of directors of Summer Seals Day Camp, a program that provides elementary school children whose reading and math skills are below grade level with the help they need in a camp-like setting. She is also a member of the steering committee for Saturday Science, a program that provides hands-on science exploration and education to children and their parents.

Before she earned her Ph.D. in English and Education at the University of Michigan in Ann Arbor, Dr. Reeves taught English and social studies at the secondary level in public schools. She is the author of *Adolescents Talk about Reading: Exploring Resistance to and Engagement with Text*. She can be reached at reeves@susqu.edu.

Related ASCD Resources: Instructional Design

At the time of publication, the following ASCD resources were available (ASCD stock numbers appear in parentheses). For up-to-date information about ASCD resources, go to www.ascd.org. You can search the complete archives of *Educational Leadership* at http://www.ascd.org/el.

ASCD Edge

Exchange ideas, look at lesson plans, and connect with other educators interested in Understanding by Design, differentiated instruction, how the brain learns, new and student teachers, the whole child, assessment for learning, and 21st century learning on the social networking site ASCD Edge™ at http://ascdedge.ascd.org/

Online Professional Development

Crafting Curriculum: An Introduction (#PD09OC25)
Crafting Curriculum: Using Standards (#PD 09OC23)
Visit the ASCD website (www.ascd.org)

Print Products

How to Plan Rigorous Instruction (Mastering the Principles of Great Teaching Series) by Robyn R. Jackson (#110077)

Making Standards Useful in the Classroom by Robert J. Marzano and Mark W. Haystead (#108006)

The Purposeful Classroom: How to Structure Lessons with Learning Goals in Mind by Douglas Fisher and Nancy Frey (#112007)

The Understanding by Design Guide to Creating High-Quality Units by Grant Wiggins and Jay McTighe (#109107)

Understanding Common Core State Standards by John S. Kendall (#112011)

Videos

Moving Forward with Understanding by Design DVD and Facilitator's Guide (#607012)
Understanding by Design DVD (3 DVD set) (#600241)

THE WHOLE CHILD The Whole Child Initiative helps schools and communities create learning environments that allow students to be healthy, safe, engaged, supported, and challenged. To learn more about other books and resources that relate to the whole child, visit www.wholechildeducation.org.

For more information: send e-mail to member@ascd.org; call 1-800-933-2723 or 703-578-9600, press 2; send a fax to 703-575-5400; or write to Information Services, ASCD, 1703 N. Beauregard St., Alexandria, VA 22311-1714 USA.